New Dimensions of Indian Education: From Tradition to Innovation

New Dimensions of Indian Education:

From Tradition to Innovation

New Dimensions of Indian Education: From Tradition to Innovation

Published By: Wissira Research Lab LLC

Imprint Name: Wissira Press

US Office: Carmel, United States- 46074

India Office: KDP, RNE, India-201017

Email: editor@wissira.us, Website: https://books.wissira.us

Mobile: +91 7535 916 555

Dr Shubhra Chaturvedi

ISBN - 978-93-7559-890-9

Maharaja Agrasen Himalayan Garhwal University,

Address: Uttarakhand, India

Edition: 2026

Printed In: India

Maharaja Agrasen Himalayan Garhwal University,

Address: Uttarakhand, India

New Dimensions of Indian Education:

From Tradition to Innovation

2026

Author:

Dr Shubhra Chaturvedi

Published By

Wissira Research Lab

ISBN 978-93-7559-890-9

Preface

Education in India has never been a static enterprise; it has evolved continuously in response to changing social realities, cultural values, political structures, and technological advancements. From the reflective and value-oriented traditions of ancient learning to the digitally mediated classrooms of the present day, Indian education reflects a long journey of adaptation, resilience, and reinvention. Rooted in a civilizational ethos that viewed knowledge as a path to self-realization and social harmony, Indian education has historically emphasized wisdom, ethics, and holistic growth. Over centuries, this system has encountered transformation through interaction with diverse cultures, colonial interventions, and modern state-led reforms. This book, *New Dimensions of Indian Education: From Tradition to Innovation*, seeks to trace that journey while critically examining how the past informs the present and shapes the future.

The motivation behind this work arises from the need to view Indian education not merely as a system of institutions, examinations, and policies, but as a living social process deeply embedded in everyday life. Education in India has traditionally been linked with moral development, community responsibility, and cultural continuity, playing a vital role in shaping collective identity. In contrast, the contemporary educational landscape is shaped by forces such as globalization, technological disruption, market-oriented skill demands, and widening equity gaps. These shifts have introduced new expectations from education—ranging from employability and innovation to digital literacy and lifelong learning. This book attempts to bridge these dimensions by presenting education as both a cultural inheritance and a dynamic tool for national development and global engagement.

Each chapter has been carefully designed to offer a balanced, analytical, and reflective perspective. The early chapters explore the philosophical and historical foundations of Indian education, highlighting how ancient and medieval systems prioritized holistic development, ethical reasoning, dialogue-based learning, and the transmission of knowledge across generations. The discussion then moves to the colonial period, examining how formalized schooling structures reshaped curricula, language policies, and access to education. Post-independence reforms, constitutional commitments, and policy initiatives are subsequently analysed to understand India's efforts to democratize education and align it with developmental goals. The later sections focus on innovation, addressing themes such as digital learning ecosystems, teacher empowerment, inclusive education, multilingualism, and the future of Indian education within an increasingly interconnected global knowledge economy.

This book is intended for a wide and diverse readership, including students, educators, researchers, policymakers, and readers interested in understanding the evolving landscape of Indian education. Care has been taken to ensure that the content remains academically rigorous yet accessible, grounded in authentic scholarship, and free from plagiarism. Rather than prescribing rigid solutions or singular viewpoints, the book encourages reflection, dialogue, and critical engagement with educational change across social, cultural, and institutional contexts.

Ultimately, *New Dimensions of Indian Education: From Tradition to Innovation* aspires to contribute meaningfully to ongoing conversations about how education can honour India's rich intellectual and cultural heritage while equipping learners to navigate an increasingly complex and uncertain world. It is hoped that this work will inspire thoughtful inquiry, informed policymaking, and responsible action toward building an education system that is inclusive, innovative, adaptable, and deeply rooted in human values.

Author:

Dr Shubhra Chaturvedi

Overview of the Book

New Dimensions of Indian Education: From Tradition to Innovation presents a comprehensive and critically informed exploration of the historical evolution, structural transformation, and emerging future of education in India. The book is grounded in the understanding that education is not merely an institutional arrangement or a mechanism for skill acquisition, but a dynamic social, cultural, and ethical force that shapes individual identity, collective consciousness, and national development. Education is examined as a living system—one that reflects societal values, power structures, and aspirations while continuously adapting to changing economic, technological, and demographic realities. By tracing the journey of Indian education across time, the book highlights how enduring civilizational traditions continue to inform modern reforms, policy choices, and pedagogical innovations.

The opening chapters examine the philosophical and pedagogical foundations of education in ancient and medieval India, drawing attention to the integral relationship between knowledge, character formation, and social responsibility. These sections emphasize the holistic nature of early learning systems, where education was embedded in everyday life and closely aligned with moral reasoning, experiential learning, and dialogue-based inquiry. Gurukul and madrasah traditions are discussed not merely as historical institutions, but as knowledge ecosystems that valued interdisciplinarity, mentorship, and intellectual autonomy. The discussion then transitions to the colonial period, analysing how external influences restructured educational priorities, introduced standardized schooling models, and redefined the purpose of education in relation to administration, employment, and social stratification. This shift is critically examined for its long-term impact on curriculum design, language hierarchies, and access to educational opportunities.

The middle chapters focus on post-independence reforms and contemporary policy transformations, situating education as a central pillar of nation-building, democratic participation, and socio-economic mobility. The expansion of public education, efforts toward universal literacy, and the role of higher education in scientific and technological advancement are explored in detail. Key themes include the pursuit of equity and inclusion, the challenges of regional and socio-economic disparities, and the gradual shift toward learner-centric, outcomes-based, and competency-driven education frameworks. National education policies are critically examined for their role in redefining curriculum structures, assessment systems, institutional governance, and teacher accountability, while also addressing implementation gaps and systemic constraints.

In its later sections, the book addresses the transformative impact of technology, pedagogy, and globalization on Indian education. Digital learning ecosystems blended, and online education models, teacher professional development, inclusive and multilingual education, and lifelong learning emerge as defining features of contemporary educational practice. The book also explores the ethical and social implications of educational technology, emphasizing the need for human-Centered design and equitable access. The final chapter situates Indian education within the global knowledge economy, examining how research, innovation, entrepreneurship, and international collaboration can coexist with cultural continuity, social responsibility, and ethical integrity.

Overall, this book offers an integrated and forward-looking perspective on Indian education. It serves both as a reflective account of India's educational heritage and as a strategic guide for future development. By thoughtfully connecting tradition with innovation, policy with practice, and local realities with global trends, the book provides readers with a nuanced understanding of how education in India can remain socially grounded, globally relevant, and responsive to the evolving needs of a rapidly changing world

Table of Contents

1

Foundations of Indian Education in Ancient Civilization

1.1 Philosophical Roots of Learning in Ancient India

Ancient Indian education was deeply grounded in philosophy, viewing knowledge as a path to self-realization rather than mere skill acquisition. Learning aimed at understanding *dharma* (ethical duty), *artha* (material responsibility), *kama* (balanced desire), and *moksha* (liberation).

In ancient India, education was not treated as a utilitarian process aimed solely at earning a livelihood. Instead, learning was understood as a lifelong journey toward inner growth, ethical living, and spiritual awareness. Knowledge was valued for its transformative power-its ability to refine the mind, discipline behaviour, and elevate human consciousness. Education was therefore inseparable from philosophy, spirituality, and moral responsibility.

The philosophical foundation of ancient Indian learning rested on the holistic understanding of human life, often expressed through the four purusharthas -dharma, artha, kama, and moksha. Education helped individuals understand dharma, or righteous conduct, guiding them to live ethically within society. Learners were encouraged to act responsibly, respect social harmony, and uphold justice. Artha, representing material well-being, was not rejected but taught as a pursuit that must align with moral values. Knowledge enabled individuals to earn and manage resources without greed or exploitation.

Kama, or balanced desire, highlighted the importance of emotional regulation and moderation. Education cultivated self-control, teaching learners to enjoy life without excess or attachment. Above all, moksha, or liberation, was regarded as the highest goal of learning. Intellectual inquiry, reflection, and meditation were encouraged as paths toward self-realization and freedom from ignorance.

Ancient Indian education also placed strong emphasis on **character formation**. Moral discipline, humility, truthfulness, and respect for teachers and society were considered essential outcomes of learning. The teacher–student relationship was deeply personal, focusing on mentorship rather than instruction alone. Knowledge was transmitted through dialogue, reflection, and lived experience, ensuring that wisdom was internalized rather than memorized.

Overall, the philosophical roots of learning in ancient India reveal an education system designed to develop the whole person-intellectually, morally, socially, and spiritually making learning a means of personal refinement and collective well-being rather than mere professional preparation.

1.2 The Gurukul System and Holistic Development

The Gurukul system represented a residential model of education where students lived with their teacher in a simple environment. Learning was experiential, dialogic, and individualized.

The Gurukul system was a distinctive educational model in ancient India that emphasized immersive and holistic learning rather than formal classroom instruction. In this system, students resided in the household of their teacher, creating a close-knit learning community. Education unfolded within a simple and disciplined environment, where daily life itself became a medium of learning. This residential arrangement allowed education to extend beyond fixed hours, integrating learning seamlessly into everyday activities.

Instruction in the Gurukul system was highly **experiential and personalized**. Instead of standardized curricula, teaching was adapted to each student's abilities, interests, and pace of understanding. Knowledge was transmitted through oral discussions, observation, questioning, and reflective dialogue. This interactive approach encouraged critical thinking, deep comprehension, and intellectual independence rather than rote memorization.

A defining feature of the Gurukul system was its strong focus on **character and life skills**. Students actively participated in household duties such as cooking, cleaning, collecting resources, and caring for the environment. These activities cultivated self-reliance, discipline, humility, and a sense of responsibility. Learning through service reinforced the idea that knowledge carried social obligations and should contribute to collective well-being.

Emotional and social development were equally important outcomes of Gurukul education. Living together fostered cooperation, empathy, and respect among students from diverse backgrounds. The close teacher–student bond promoted trust, moral guidance, and emotional maturity. Teachers acted not only as instructors but also as mentors and role models, shaping attitudes and values through personal example.

Overall, the Gurukul system nurtured the **whole individual** -intellectually, morally, emotionally, and socially. By integrating learning with daily life and ethical practice, it instilled a lifelong respect for knowledge and personal growth. This holistic approach ensured that education prepared individuals not just for professional roles, but for meaningful and responsible participation in society.

1.3 Curriculum, Methods, and Knowledge Domains

Ancient Indian education covered a wide range of disciplines including philosophy, mathematics, astronomy, medicine, linguistics, and the arts. Teaching relied on oral transmission, memorization, debate, and reflective inquiry.

The curriculum of ancient Indian education was remarkably broad and integrative, reflecting the belief that true learning must address multiple dimensions of human understanding. Education did not confine itself to a single discipline but embraced philosophy, mathematics, astronomy, medicine, linguistics, logic, music, fine arts, and practical sciences. This diversity ensured that learners developed both abstract reasoning and applied knowledge, enabling them to understand the world intellectually as well as experientially.

Teaching methods were primarily **oral and interactive**, as knowledge was preserved and transmitted through spoken word rather than written texts. Memorization played an important role, especially in mastering complex philosophical ideas, mathematical formulas, and linguistic structures. However, memorization was not mechanical; it was supported by meaning, rhythm, and repetition, helping students internalize knowledge deeply and accurately.

Debate and discussion were central to the learning process. Students were encouraged to engage in logical arguments, challenge assumptions, and defend their viewpoints using reasoned evidence. This practice sharpened analytical skills and nurtured intellectual confidence. Reflective inquiry-thinking deeply about ideas and their implications-allowed learners to connect knowledge with personal experience and ethical understanding.

Storytelling and questioning were powerful pedagogical tools. Teachers often used narratives, metaphors, and real-life examples to explain complex concepts, making learning engaging and accessible. Question-based teaching promoted curiosity and independent thinking, guiding students to discover insights rather than passively receive information.

Importantly, ancient Indian education was **learner-centred** rather than standardized. Instruction was adapted to individual abilities, interests, and aptitudes. Students progressed at their own pace, allowing intellectual diversity to thrive. This flexible approach recognized that learning is not uniform and that each individual contributes uniquely to the collective pursuit of knowledge.

1.4 Social Purpose and Ethical Orientation of Education

Education in ancient India was viewed as a social responsibility rather than a commercial activity. Knowledge was shared freely, and learning was meant to serve society. Ethical conduct, compassion, and social harmony were central outcomes. Although access was shaped by social structures of the time, the underlying ideal emphasized wisdom, restraint, and service to the community.

In ancient India, education was fundamentally regarded as a **social and moral obligation**, not a profit-driven enterprise. The transmission of knowledge was considered a sacred duty of the learned, undertaken for the welfare of society as a whole. Teachers imparted education as a service, and students received it with a sense of responsibility, gratitude, and commitment to use learning for constructive purposes. The value of education lay not in economic gain alone, but in its capacity to sustain social order and ethical living.

A core objective of education was the cultivation of **ethical conduct and inner discipline** . Learners were trained to develop qualities such as honesty, compassion, self-restraint, and respect for others. Intellectual growth was inseparable from moral development, as knowledge without ethics was viewed as incomplete or even harmful. Education aimed to shape individuals who could act wisely, resolve conflicts peacefully, and contribute to social harmony.

The social orientation of education emphasized **service to the community** . Learners were encouraged to apply their knowledge in ways that benefited others-whether through teaching, healing, governance, or creative expression. Education prepared individuals to fulfil social roles responsibly, reinforcing the idea that personal advancement should align with collective well-being.

While access to education was influenced by the social structures of the time, the philosophical ideal behind learning stressed **wisdom over privilege** . True education was believed to cultivate humility rather than arrogance and responsibility rather than dominance. Restraint in desire, balance in action, and service-mindedness were upheld as markers of genuine learning.

Overall, ancient Indian education was ethically oriented and socially purposeful. It sought to create thoughtful, morally grounded individuals whose knowledge strengthened social cohesion and upheld shared values, ensuring that learning functioned as a force for stability, justice, and communal progress.

Social Purpose &
Ethical Orientation of Education
Wisdom
Ethical Conduct
Service

Aspect of Education	Core Emphasis	Intended Outcome
Social responsibility	Education as a duty to society, not a commercial activity	Knowledge used for collective welfare
Ethical conduct	Emphasis on honesty, self-restraint, and moral discipline	Development of virtuous individuals
Compassion and harmony	Encouraging empathy, cooperation, and social balance	Peaceful and cohesive communities
Service-oriented learning	Applying knowledge through teaching, healing, and governance	Social upliftment and responsibility
Wisdom over privilege	Valuing humility and insight rather than status	Ethical leadership and social justice
Community contribution	Learning linked to societal roles and obligations	Sustainable social development

Multiple-Choice Questions (MCQs)

1. What was the primary aim of education in ancient India?

A. Preparation for government employment
B. Accumulation of material wealth

C. Self-realization and ethical living
D. Mastery of technical skills only
Answer: C. Self-realization and ethical living

2. The Gurukul system is best described as:

A. A centralized school system with fixed curricula
B. A residential model where students lived with the teacher
C. An examination-based education framework
D. A commercial institution for professional training
Answer: B. A residential model where students lived with the teacher

3. Which teaching method was most commonly used in ancient Indian education?

A. Printed textbooks and written exams
B. Online learning and simulations
C. Oral transmission through dialogue and memorization
D. Audio-visual instruction
Answer: C. Oral transmission through dialogue and memorization

4. Which of the following was NOT a central value promoted by ancient Indian education?

A. Ethical conduct
B. Social responsibility
C. Competitive individualism
D. Service to society
Answer: C. Competitive individualism

5. Why was education considered a social responsibility in ancient India?

A. It was funded by the state
B. Knowledge was meant to serve community welfare
C. Teachers were paid by students

D. Learning was restricted to elites

Answer: B. Knowledge was meant to serve community welfare

Short Answer Questions

1. What philosophical purpose did education serve in ancient Indian civilization?
2. Briefly explain the Gurukul system of education.
3. How did ethical values shape the goals of ancient Indian education?
4. What role did oral transmission play in ancient learning methods?
5. Why was education considered a social responsibility rather than a commercial activity?
6. How did ancient Indian education support holistic development of learners?

Long-Answer Questions

1. Discuss the philosophical foundations of education in ancient India with reference to dharma, artha, kama, and moksha.
2. Explain the structure and significance of the Gurukul system in promoting holistic development.
3. Describe the curriculum and teaching methods used in ancient Indian education and their impact on intellectual growth.
4. Analyse the social purpose and ethical orientation of education in ancient Indian civilization.
5. Examine how learner-centred education allowed intellectual diversity to flourish in ancient India.
6. Critically evaluate the relevance of ancient Indian educational principles in the modern education system.

2

Medieval Transformations and Knowledge Transmission

2.1 Institutional Expansion and Educational Diversity

The medieval period saw the emergence of new educational institutions such as madrasas, pathshalas, and monastic centres. These institutions expanded access to learning and supported specialized instruction. Education became more structured while still preserving oral and manuscript-based traditions.

During the medieval period, Indian education experienced significant institutional growth, marked by the emergence and consolidation of diverse centres of learning such as **madrasas, pathshalas,** and **monastic institutions**. These establishments reflected the pluralistic social and cultural landscape of the time and played a crucial role in broadening access to education beyond earlier, more localized systems. Learning was no longer confined to a single tradition or method; instead, multiple institutions coexisted, each addressing the intellectual and spiritual needs of different communities.

Madrasas introduced a more organized form of education, emphasizing subjects such as theology, law, philosophy, mathematics, astronomy, and language studies. Their structured curricula, regular teaching schedules, and evaluation methods contributed to greater academic discipline and continuity. Pathshalas, on the other hand, continued to serve as community-based institutions where foundational learning in language, arithmetic, ethics, and cultural practices was imparted, often in regional languages. Monastic centres-both Hindu and Buddhist-functioned as hubs of advanced learning, preserving classical texts and encouraging scholarly debate.

Despite increased institutional organization, education during this period retained strong oral traditions. Knowledge transmission relied heavily on memorization, recitation, and dialogue between teacher and student, complemented by handwritten manuscripts that safeguarded intellectual heritage. This balance between structure and tradition ensured that learning remained accessible, adaptable, and rooted in cultural values.

2.2 Multilingual Scholarship and Cultural Exchange

Education during this period was marked by linguistic diversity. Sanskrit, Persian, Arabic, and regional languages coexisted as mediums of instruction. Scholars translated texts across languages, facilitating cross-cultural knowledge exchange.

Education in the medieval period of India was characterized by rich linguistic plurality, reflecting the region's cultural and intellectual diversity. Multiple languages-classical, scholarly, and vernacular-functioned simultaneously as mediums of instruction, enabling learning to reach a wide range of communities. Rather than replacing one another, these languages coexisted and interacted, creating a dynamic environment of knowledge production and exchange.

Sanskrit continued to serve as a key language for philosophy, science, grammar, and classical literature, preserving long-established intellectual traditions. At the same time, Persian and Arabic gained prominence, particularly in fields such as administration, law, history, medicine, astronomy, and theology. Regional languages also played an important role in education, especially in transmitting practical knowledge, moral instruction, poetry, and local histories to broader sections of society. This multilingual framework ensured that education was not restricted to a single linguistic or cultural group.

A defining feature of this period was the active translation of texts across languages. Scholars translated works on mathematics, medicine, astronomy, philosophy, and ethics, allowing ideas to travel between cultural and intellectual traditions. Through translation and commentary, concepts were not merely copied but interpreted and adapted to new contexts. This process encouraged dialogue between different knowledge systems and expanded the scope of learning.

Overall, multilingual scholarship strengthened cultural exchange and intellectual enrichment. The interaction of languages facilitated mutual influence, innovation, and synthesis of ideas, helping Indian education evolve as an inclusive and interconnected system rather than a rigid or isolated one.

Language	Primary Domains of Study	Role in Education and Scholarship	Contribution to Cultural Exchange
Sanskrit	Philosophy, grammar, science, literature, logic	Preserved classical knowledge and intellectual rigor	Served as a foundation for translations and reinterpretations
Persian	Administration, history, poetry, law	Introduced structured documentation and historiography	Linked Indian scholarship with Central Asian and Persian traditions
Arabic	Medicine, astronomy, mathematics, theology	Expanded scientific and medical learning	Facilitated transmission of global scientific ideas
Regional Languages	Ethics, folklore, poetry, practical education	Made education accessible to wider society	Enabled localization and popularization of knowledge

2.3 Advancements in Science, Arts, and Humanities

Significant progress occurred in mathematics, astronomy, architecture, medicine, and literature. Educational centres became hubs for research

and innovation. Learning was often patronized by rulers and supported through endowments, enabling scholars to pursue advanced inquiry.

The medieval period in India witnessed notable advancements across science, arts, and the humanities, reflecting a mature and evolving educational ecosystem. Learning during this era moved beyond basic transmission of knowledge and increasingly emphasized inquiry, experimentation, and creative expression. Fields such as mathematics, astronomy, medicine, architecture, and literature flourished as scholars engaged deeply with both inherited knowledge and contemporary challenges.

Mathematics and astronomy advanced through refined numerical methods, observational techniques, and theoretical models used for calendrical calculations, navigation, and ritual planning. Medical education expanded through systematic study of anatomy, herbal knowledge, diagnostics, and surgical practices, often combining empirical observation with classical texts. Architecture and the arts benefited from applied scientific understanding, resulting in sophisticated construction techniques, urban planning, sculpture, and decorative arts that blended aesthetics with engineering precision. Literature and the humanities thrived through poetry, historical writing, philosophy, and linguistic studies, enriching cultural expression and intellectual discourse.

Educational centres such as madrasas, monastic institutions, and scholarly courts functioned as hubs of research and innovation. These spaces encouraged debate, commentary, and original contributions rather than rote learning alone. Crucially, many rulers and elites actively patronized education by providing grants, land endowments, and institutional support. This patronage allowed scholars to dedicate themselves fully to advanced study, teaching, and research without constant material constraints.

A defining strength of this period was the close integration of theory and practice. Knowledge was not confined to abstract ideas but was tested and applied in real-world contexts-whether in medical treatment, architectural design, artistic production, or administrative problem-solving. This balance strengthened applied learning and ensured that education remained socially relevant, practical, and innovative, leaving a lasting impact on India's intellectual and cultural heritage.

2.4 Education as a Social and Administrative Tool

Education increasingly served administrative and governance needs, producing scholars, record keepers, judges, and advisors. While intellectual inquiry continued, education also aligned with state functions.

During the medieval period, education gradually assumed a more pragmatic role by aligning itself with the administrative and governance requirements of the state. While learning had long been valued for moral, spiritual, and intellectual growth, it now also became an essential means of preparing individuals for public service. Educational institutions contributed directly to the functioning of governance by training professionals who could manage records, interpret laws, advise rulers, and administer justice.

Scholars educated in languages, law, accounting, and ethics were increasingly employed as administrators, judges, scribes, and counsellors. Mastery of writing systems, documentation practices, and legal reasoning became crucial skills, especially as states expanded and governance grew more complex. Education thus supported the creation of an efficient administrative structure, ensuring continuity, accountability, and informed decision-making within political systems.

Despite this functional shift, intellectual inquiry did not disappear. Philosophical reflection, literary production, and scientific study continued alongside vocational training. Educational curricula often balanced theoretical understanding with practical application, allowing learners to engage with abstract ideas while also acquiring skills relevant to societal roles. This dual focus ensured that education did not become purely utilitarian or narrowly technical.

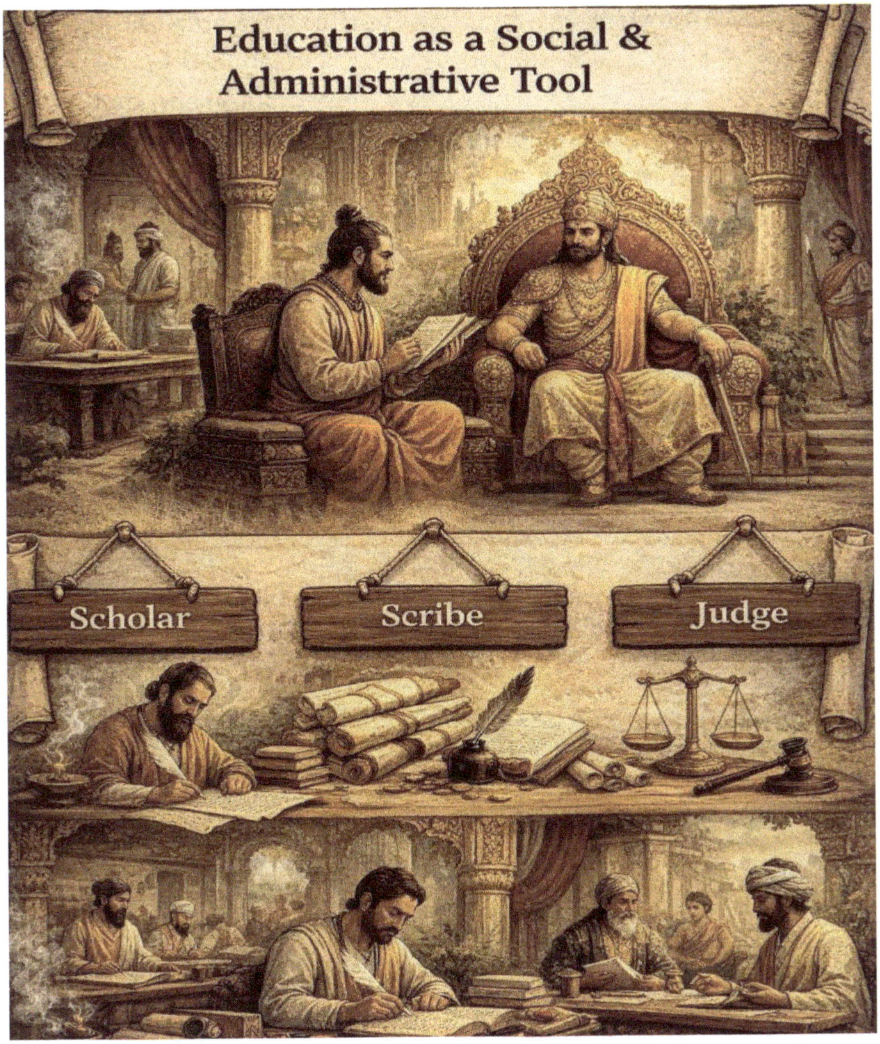

Overall, the use of education as a social and administrative tool reflects a thoughtful balance between idealism and utility. Learning remained rooted in scholarly traditions and ethical considerations, even as it adapted to meet the evolving needs of society and governance. This balance strengthened the relevance of education while preserving its deeper intellectual and cultural foundations.

Example: Education Supporting Medieval Administration

In a medieval kingdom, an educational institution located near the royal court played a key role in supporting governance. Students trained there studied subjects such as language, law, ethics, arithmetic, and record-keeping. Their education emphasized clarity of writing, logical reasoning, and familiarity with legal and administrative procedures. This preparation enabled graduates to serve effectively in public roles.

After completing their studies, many learners were appointed as scribes, accountants, judges, or advisors. Scribes maintained land records, tax registers, and official correspondence, ensuring administrative continuity. Judges applied legal principles learned through texts and case discussions to resolve disputes fairly. Advisors used their scholarly training to guide rulers on ethical governance, policy decisions, and social welfare matters.

At the same time, these officials remained connected to scholarly traditions. Many continued to study philosophy, literature, or religious texts alongside their administrative duties. This ensured that governance was not only efficient but also informed by ethical reasoning and intellectual depth.

This example illustrates how medieval education balanced practical state needs with enduring scholarly values, making learning both socially useful and intellectually grounded.

Multiple Choice Questions (MCQs)

1. Which of the following institutions emerged prominently during the medieval period to expand access to education in India?

A. Gurukuls only
B. Universities modelled on European systems
C. Madrasas, pathshalas, and monastic centres
D. Industrial training schools
Answer: C

2. What was a key feature of medieval education regarding language use?

A. Exclusive use of Sanskrit for all instruction
B. Replacement of classical languages by regional languages
C. Coexistence of multiple languages as mediums of learning
D. Elimination of oral traditions
Answer: C

3. How did translation activities contribute to knowledge transmission during the medieval period?

A. By limiting knowledge to elite groups
B. By preserving texts without interpretation
C. By enabling cross-cultural exchange of ideas
D. By discouraging original scholarship
Answer: C

4. What role did royal patronage play in medieval educational advancement?

A. It restricted learning to administrative training only
B. It discouraged scientific and artistic inquiry
C. It supported scholars through grants and endowments
D. It replaced educational institutions with courts
Answer: C

5. In what way did education function as a social and administrative tool in the medieval period?

A. By focusing solely on spiritual liberation
B. By preparing individuals for governance and public service
C. By eliminating theoretical learning
D. By promoting only military training
Answer: B

Short Answer Questions

1. What types of educational institutions expanded during the medieval period in India?
2. How did multilingualism influence medieval scholarship and learning?
3. Why were translation activities important in medieval education?
4. What role did royal patronage play in supporting scholars and educational centres?

5. How was theoretical knowledge integrated with practical application during this period?
6. In what ways did education support administrative and governance needs in medieval society?

Long Answer Questions

1. Discuss the institutional expansion of education during the medieval period and explain how it contributed to educational diversity.
2. Examine the role of multilingual scholarship in facilitating cultural and intellectual exchange in medieval India.
3. Analyse the advancements in science, arts, and humanities during the medieval period and the factors that supported this progress.
4. Explain how royal patronage and endowments influenced the development of research and innovation in medieval educational centres.
5. Evaluate the role of education as a social and administrative tool while maintaining scholarly traditions.
6. Assess how medieval systems of knowledge transmission balanced oral traditions, manuscript culture, and institutional learning.

3

Colonial Influence and the Restructuring of Education

3.1 Introduction of Western Educational Models

Colonial rule introduced formal schooling systems based on Western curricula, standardized examinations, and classroom instruction. Education shifted from community-based learning to institutional frameworks.

The advent of colonial rule marked a decisive transformation in the educational landscape, as Western models of schooling were systematically introduced and institutionalized. Education, which had earlier evolved through community traditions, apprenticeships, and localized centres of learning, began to be reorganized into structured institutions such as schools, colleges, and universities. These institutions followed fixed timetables, age-based classes, prescribed syllabi, and uniform methods of instruction, emphasizing discipline, regular assessment, and formal certification. Learning was no longer embedded primarily in social or cultural contexts but was increasingly mediated through classrooms and textbooks.

A defining feature of this transformation was the adoption of Western curricula that prioritized subjects such as mathematics, natural sciences, history, geography, and political economy as understood through European intellectual traditions. Knowledge was categorized, standardized, and evaluated through written examinations, replacing earlier oral, experiential, and mentorship-based systems. This shift promoted comparability and administrative efficiency but often marginalized indigenous knowledge systems that did not fit easily into standardized frameworks.

The growing prominence of English as the medium of instruction further reshaped educational access and aspirations. English became associated with modernity, administrative employment, and social mobility, positioning it as a gateway to power and professional advancement. While this enabled sections of society to engage with global ideas and scientific developments, it also created linguistic hierarchies that distanced education from local languages and cultural expressions. Consequently, Western educational models redefined not only the structure of learning but also its underlying priorities, aligning education with bureaucratic needs, economic utility, and colonial governance rather than holistic community development.

3.2 Marginalization of Indigenous Knowledge Systems

Traditional Indian knowledge systems were often undervalued or excluded from formal education. Indigenous pedagogy, languages, and philosophical traditions were sidelined in favour of Western disciplines.

With the expansion of colonial education, long-established indigenous knowledge systems gradually lost their central place in formal learning.

Traditional forms of education in India had been deeply rooted in local contexts, drawing upon regional languages, oral traditions, lived experience, and philosophical inquiry. These systems emphasized holistic development, ethical reasoning, and practical wisdom shaped by social, environmental, and cultural realities. However, colonial educational reforms often failed to recognize these strengths, viewing indigenous knowledge as informal, unscientific, or incompatible with modern administrative needs.

Western disciplines and pedagogical methods were privileged within institutional frameworks, leaving little room for traditional subjects such as classical philosophy, local histories, medicine, astronomy, arts, and craft-based learning. Indigenous languages were increasingly excluded from formal instruction, which reduced their academic legitimacy and weakened their role as carriers of cultural memory. As a result, learners were encouraged to engage with knowledge systems that were often detached from their immediate social environment, while local intellectual traditions were pushed to the margins.

This shift produced a growing disconnect between education and everyday life. Students trained primarily in Western frameworks frequently found limited relevance between what they learned in classrooms and the realities of their communities. Over time, the reduced transmission of indigenous pedagogy led to the decline of traditional teacher–student relationships, oral scholarship, and experiential learning practices. The marginalization of indigenous knowledge thus did not merely alter educational content; it also disrupted cultural continuity, contributing to the gradual erosion of locally grounded ways of knowing and learning.

3.3 Education, Employment, and Social Mobility

Colonial education linked learning with clerical employment and administrative roles. Education became a means of social mobility for some, while reinforcing inequalities for others.

During the colonial period, education became closely tied to employment within the administrative and clerical machinery of the state. Formal schooling was designed to produce a workforce capable of assisting colonial governance, particularly in roles such as record keeping, translation, accounting, and lower-level administration. As a result, educational attainment was increasingly measured by one's ability to secure salaried employment rather than by intellectual growth or moral development. This pragmatic linkage reshaped the social meaning of education.

For certain social groups, especially those with access to English-medium institutions and urban centres, colonial education functioned as a powerful tool for upward mobility. Literacy in English and possession of recognized certificates opened pathways to government jobs, financial stability, and enhanced social status. However, this opportunity was unevenly distributed. Large sections of society-particularly rural populations and marginalized communities-remained excluded due to economic barriers, linguistic disadvantages, and limited institutional reach. Thus, while education enabled mobility for some, it simultaneously reinforced existing inequalities.

The growing emphasis on examinations, degrees, and formal credentials transformed learning into a competitive process. Success was increasingly defined by performance in standardized tests rather than depth of understanding or creative inquiry. Education gradually shifted from a pursuit of wisdom and holistic development to a means of acquiring qualifications for employment. This change altered learners' motivations, encouraging conformity and rote learning, and reoriented education toward job-oriented training rather than intellectual and ethical cultivation.

3.4 Seeds of Reform and Intellectual Awakening

Despite its limitations, colonial education also sparked critical thinking and reform movements. Exposure to new ideas encouraged debates on social justice, freedom, and national identity. Educated Indians began questioning colonial dominance and advocating educational reform, laying the groundwork for future transformations after independence.

Although colonial education imposed structural limitations and cultural hierarchies, it also unintentionally became a catalyst for intellectual awakening and reform. Exposure to Western philosophy, political thought, history, and science introduced educated Indians to ideas such as liberty, equality, constitutional governance, and human rights. These concepts encouraged critical reflection on social practices, political authority, and the legitimacy of colonial rule itself. Education thus evolved into a space where questioning and debate could emerge, even within a system designed to serve imperial interests.

Educated Indians began to apply newly acquired analytical tools to examine their own society as well as colonial governance. Social reform movements addressing issues such as caste discrimination, gender inequality, child marriage, and access to education gained momentum through educated leadership. Print culture-newspapers, journals, pamphlets, and books-expanded rapidly, enabling the spread of reformist ideas and public debate. Education fostered a new class of thinkers who combined indigenous concerns with global intellectual currents, creating a dynamic environment of critique and dialogue.

Section	Core Focus	Key Changes Introduced	Social & Cultural Impact	Long-Term Implications
3.1 Introduction of Western Educational Models	Structural transformation of education	Formal schools, Western curricula, standardized exams, classroom-based instruction, English medium	Shift from community-based learning to institutional systems; prioritization of administrative knowledge	Established modern schooling framework; redefined education as formal and credential-based

3.2 Marginalization of Indigenous Knowledge Systems	Displacement of traditional learning	Exclusion of indigenous pedagogy, languages, philosophies, and experiential learning	Cultural disconnect between education and local life; decline of traditional teacher–student models	Erosion of indigenous knowledge transmission; later revival efforts post-independence
3.3 Education, Employment, and Social Mobility	Link between education and jobs	Emphasis on clerical/administrative roles, examinations, degrees, certification	Enabled limited upward mobility; reinforced class, linguistic, and regional inequalities	Education became job-oriented and competitive; rise of credentialism

Importantly, colonial education played a role in shaping political consciousness and national identity. As Indians became aware of democratic ideals and nationalist movements abroad, they increasingly questioned foreign domination and demanded self-rule. Many leaders of reform movements and the freedom struggle emerged from this educated class, advocating both political independence and the restructuring of education to reflect indigenous values and social needs. Thus, despite its colonial constraints, the educational system planted the seeds for reform and resistance, laying the intellectual foundation for post-independence transformations in society and education.

Multiple Choice Questions (MCQs)

1. Which of the following was a major structural change introduced by colonial education in India?

A. Emphasis on oral transmission of knowledge
B. Community-based apprenticeship learning
C. Standardized curricula and examination systems
D. Religious instruction as the primary focus

Correct Answer: C

2. How did colonial education affect indigenous knowledge systems in India?

A. They were fully integrated into formal schooling
B. They were modernized and expanded
C. They were largely marginalized and excluded
D. They replaced Western disciplines

Correct Answer: C

3. The growing importance of English during the colonial period primarily led to:

A. Greater access to education for rural populations
B. Strengthening of regional languages
C. New social hierarchies based on language proficiency
D. Elimination of examination systems

Correct Answer: C

4. Colonial education linked learning most closely with which outcome?

A. Spiritual enlightenment
B. Agricultural productivity
C. Clerical and administrative employment
D. Artistic and cultural development

Correct Answer: C

5. Despite its limitations, colonial education contributed to which long-term development in India?

A. Complete rejection of Western ideas
B. Decline of political awareness
C. Intellectual awakening and reform movements
D. Elimination of social inequalities

Correct Answer: C

Short Answer Questions

1. What were the key features of Western educational models introduced during colonial rule?
2. How did the use of English as a medium of instruction affect access to education in colonial India?
3. In what ways were indigenous knowledge systems marginalized under colonial education?
4. Why did colonial education emphasize examinations and certification?
5. How did education become linked with employment during the colonial period?
6. What role did colonial education play in shaping early reformist thinking in India?

Long Answer Questions

1. Examine the transformation of India's traditional education system under colonial rule, highlighting the shift from community-based learning to institutional frameworks.

2. Discuss the impact of colonial education on indigenous knowledge systems, languages, and pedagogical practices.

3. Analyse how colonial education contributed to social mobility while simultaneously reinforcing social and economic inequalities.

4. Evaluate the role of English-language education in reshaping Indian society and intellectual life during the colonial period.

5. Critically assess how the examination-oriented and credential-based nature of colonial education altered the purpose of learning in India.

6. "Colonial education planted the seeds of reform and resistance." Discuss this statement with reference to intellectual awakening, social reform movements, and the rise of national consciousness.

4

Post-Independence Educational Reforms and Nation Building

4.1 Education as a Tool for National Reconstruction

After independence, education was viewed as a critical instrument for rebuilding the nation and shaping a democratic society. Policymakers emphasized education as a means to foster national unity, social cohesion, and scientific thinking.

In the years following independence, education assumed a central role in the project of national reconstruction. The newly sovereign nation faced the immense task of unifying a socially, linguistically, and economically diverse population while overcoming the structural legacies of colonial rule. Education was therefore not seen merely as a system for imparting literacy or vocational skills, but as a foundational mechanism for shaping a shared national consciousness and democratic ethos.

Post-independence educational thinking emphasized the creation of informed and responsible citizens. Schools and universities were expected to nurture values such as equality, secularism, tolerance, and civic responsibility. Through curricula that highlighted constitutional principles, national history, and collective aspirations, education became a medium through which individuals could understand their role within a democratic framework. This approach aimed to strengthen social cohesion by encouraging mutual respect across regions, languages, and communities.

At the same time, education was closely linked to economic development and modernization. Policymakers recognized that scientific temper, technical knowledge, and rational thinking were essential for transforming an agrarian economy into a self-reliant and industrializing nation.

Institutions of higher learning, research centres, and technical schools were expanded to produce skilled professionals capable of contributing to infrastructure development, healthcare, governance, and industry. Education thus functioned as a catalyst for both intellectual and material progress.

Importantly, post-independence education was also envisioned as a corrective force for social inequalities. By widening access to schooling and promoting inclusive policies, education was expected to empower marginalized groups and support social mobility. In this sense, education became a moral and strategic investment in the future-shaping citizens who could participate meaningfully in democracy, contribute to national development, and uphold the ideals of unity and social harmony that underpinned the nation-building process.

Example: Expansion of Public Education and National Institutions after Independence

A clear example of education being used as a tool for national reconstruction is the establishment and expansion of public educational institutions in India after 1947. The government invested heavily in building schools, universities, and specialized institutes to support nation-building goals. Institutions such as the Indian Institutes of Technology (IITs) were created to develop scientific and technical expertise needed for industrial growth and self-reliance. These institutions were not only centres of learning but symbols of a modern, forward-looking nation.

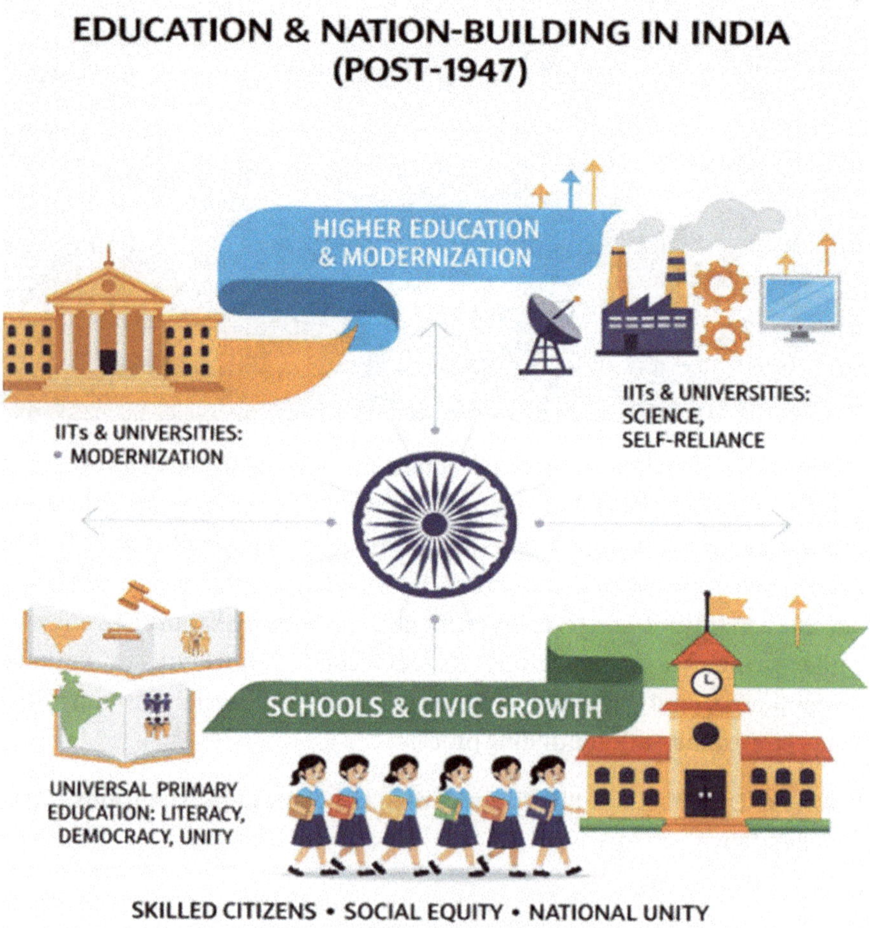

At the school level, curricula were redesigned to emphasize national history, constitutional values, and civic responsibility. Subjects like social studies and civics helped students understand democracy, fundamental rights, and duties, fostering a sense of shared identity and participation in public life. Simultaneously, programs promoting universal primary education aimed to reduce illiteracy and social inequality, enabling broader sections of society to contribute to economic and social development.

Through these initiatives, education directly supported national reconstruction by producing skilled professionals, informed citizens, and socially conscious individuals aligned with the goals of democracy, unity, and development.

4.2 Expansion of Formal Education Systems

Post-independence India witnessed rapid expansion in schools, colleges, and universities. Efforts were made to increase literacy, establish public universities, and strengthen technical and professional education.

In the post-independence period, India undertook an ambitious expansion of its formal education system to address widespread illiteracy and meet the developmental needs of a newly independent nation. Large-scale efforts were directed toward opening primary and secondary schools, founding public universities, and strengthening colleges across states. This expansion reflected the belief that broad access to education was essential for democratic participation, economic progress, and social transformation.

A major priority during this phase was improving literacy levels among the general population. Government-led initiatives focused on enrolling children from diverse social and economic backgrounds, including those in rural and previously underserved regions. At the higher education level, new universities and affiliated colleges were established to accommodate the growing number of students completing secondary education. Parallelly, technical and professional education received increased attention to support industrialization, scientific research, healthcare, and administrative capacity.

Despite these achievements, the rapid growth of institutions exposed significant structural challenges. Infrastructure often lagged behind enrolment growth, resulting in overcrowded classrooms, limited laboratory facilities, and inadequate learning resources. Shortages of trained and qualified teachers further affected instructional quality, particularly in rural and remote areas. Regional disparities also persisted, with some states progressing faster than others in terms of educational access and outcomes.

This phase thus revealed an ongoing tension between quantity and quality. While the expansion succeeded in bringing millions into the formal education system, it also highlighted the need for sustained investment in teacher training, infrastructure development, and academic standards. The experience underscored that educational growth must balance accessibility with quality to ensure that expansion translates into meaningful learning and long-term national development.

4.3 Equity, Access, and Social Justice in Education

Educational reforms increasingly emphasized inclusion of marginalized communities, women, and rural populations. Policies aimed to reduce social inequalities through reservations, scholarships, and targeted programs.

In the post-independence era, educational policy in India gradually shifted from a sole focus on expansion toward concerns of equity, access, and social justice. Recognizing that historical disadvantages had excluded large sections of society from formal learning, the state began to view education as a corrective mechanism for social inequality. Marginalized communities, women, and rural populations became central to reform agendas aimed at creating a more inclusive educational landscape.

A range of policy instruments was introduced to widen participation. Reservation policies in educational institutions sought to ensure representation of historically disadvantaged social groups, while scholarships, fee concessions, and hostel facilities helped reduce economic barriers to schooling. Special programs targeted rural and remote areas where access to quality education had long been limited. For women, initiatives focused on improving enrolment, retention, and safety, acknowledging education as a key driver of empowerment and social change.

These measures significantly expanded access and enabled education to function as a pathway for social mobility. Many individuals from disadvantaged backgrounds were able to acquire qualifications that improved employment prospects and social status. Education thus played an important role in reshaping aspirations and breaking cycles of intergenerational disadvantage.

However, disparities in learning outcomes revealed the limitations of access-focused reforms. Differences in school quality, teaching standards, language barriers, and socio-economic conditions continued to influence educational achievement. High enrolment figures did not always translate into meaningful learning or equal opportunities. This gap highlighted the need for deeper structural reforms addressing curriculum relevance, teacher preparation, institutional accountability, and broader social conditions. As a result, equity in education came to be understood not only as equal access, but as the provision of fair and supportive learning environments that enable all learners to succeed.

Case Study: Reservation and Scholarship Policies in Higher Education

A relevant case study illustrating equity, access, and social justice in education is the implementation of reservation and scholarship policies in India's higher education system after independence. These measures were introduced to address historical exclusion faced by Scheduled Castes (SC), Scheduled Tribes (ST), and later Other Backward Classes (OBC), who had limited access to formal education due to social and economic disadvantages.

Through constitutionally backed reservation policies, a fixed proportion of seats in public universities and professional institutions were allocated to students from these communities. Complementary scholarship schemes covered tuition fees, provided stipends, and supported accommodation, enabling students from low-income families to continue their education without severe financial burden. As a result, enrolment of students from marginalized backgrounds increased significantly, particularly in universities, engineering colleges, and medical institutions.

This intervention enabled many first-generation learners to access higher education and secure professional employment, contributing to upward social mobility and broader representation in skilled sectors. Graduates from these communities increasingly entered public services, academia, healthcare, and technical fields, challenging traditional patterns of exclusion.

4.4 Balancing Cultural Identity and Modern Knowledge

Post-independence education sought to integrate India's cultural heritage with modern scientific and technological learning. Curricula attempted to preserve indigenous values while promoting rational inquiry and innovation. This balancing act reflected India's broader struggle to modernize without losing its cultural and ethical foundations.

In the post-independence period, India's education system faced the complex challenge of harmonizing cultural continuity with the demands of modern knowledge. Nation-building required scientific advancement, technological capability, and rational thinking, yet there was also a strong desire to preserve India's rich philosophical, ethical, and cultural traditions. Education thus became a space where tradition and modernity were expected to coexist rather than compete.

Curriculum frameworks increasingly sought to reflect this dual purpose. Alongside mathematics, science, and technical subjects, students were introduced to Indian history, philosophy, literature, and moral education. Indigenous knowledge systems-such as traditional practices in medicine, ecology, arts, and ethics-were presented as valuable intellectual resources rather than relics of the past. This approach aimed to cultivate a sense of cultural rootedness while encouraging openness to global scientific ideas and innovation.

At the same time, modern education emphasized critical thinking, experimentation, and evidence-based reasoning. Scientific temper was promoted as essential for economic development and social progress. By encouraging inquiry and scepticism, education attempted to move learners beyond rote learning and unquestioned tradition. The challenge lay in ensuring that respect for cultural heritage did not inhibit questioning, creativity, or technological advancement.

This balancing act mirrored India's broader developmental journey. Education was expected to produce individuals who were technologically competent yet ethically grounded, modern in outlook yet culturally conscious. While tensions persisted-such as debates over language, curriculum content, and pedagogical priorities-the post-independence education system reflected an ongoing effort to modernize without erasing identity. In this sense, education functioned as both a bridge to the future and a safeguard of cultural continuity.

Dimension	Emphasis on Cultural Identity	Emphasis on Modern Knowledge
Curriculum Content	Indian history, philosophy, literature, ethics, and indigenous traditions	Science, mathematics, technology, economics, and global knowledge systems
Educational Purpose	Preservation of cultural values, moral development, and national identity	Economic development, innovation, scientific temper, and global competitiveness
Teaching Approach	Value-based learning, storytelling, classical texts, and cultural practices	Inquiry-based learning, experimentation, critical thinking, and problem solving
Knowledge Orientation	Contextual and tradition-rooted understanding of society and nature	Evidence-based, analytical, and technology-driven understanding
Learner Outcome	Culturally aware, ethically grounded, and socially responsible citizens	Skilled, rational, and adaptable individuals capable of innovation
Core Challenge	Risk of stagnation or resistance to change if tradition is uncritical	Risk of cultural alienation if modernity ignores ethical and cultural roots

Multiple Choice Questions (MCQs)

1. What was the primary objective of education in post-independence India?

A. To promote colonial administrative efficiency
B. To preserve only traditional knowledge systems
C. To support nation-building, democracy, and development
D. To limit access to higher education

Answer: C

2. Which major challenge emerged due to the rapid expansion of formal education systems after independence?

A. Decline in student enrolment
B. Excessive privatization of education
C. Tension between access and quality
D. Elimination of regional disparities

Answer: C

3. Policies such as reservations and scholarships were primarily introduced to address which concern?

A. Technological advancement
B. Social equity and inclusion
C. Administrative efficiency
D. Cultural preservation

Answer: B

4. In post-independence education, what did balancing cultural identity and modern knowledge aim to achieve?

A. Replacing tradition with science
B. Rejecting global knowledge systems
C. Integrating ethical heritage with scientific thinking
D. Limiting innovation to cultural studies

Answer: C

5. Why did increased enrolment not always result in equal learning outcomes?

A. Lack of student interest
B. Uniform teaching methods across regions
C. Structural inequalities in resources and quality
D. Overemphasis on cultural education

Answer: C

Short Answer Questions

1. Why was education considered essential for nation-building after independence?
2. What role did formal education play in promoting democratic values in post-independence India?
3. Mention two challenges faced during the rapid expansion of educational institutions after independence.
4. How did reservation and scholarship policies aim to improve educational equity?
5. What is meant by the balance between cultural identity and modern knowledge in education?
6. Why is access to education alone insufficient to achieve social justice?

Long Answer Questions

1. Discuss education as a tool for national reconstruction in post-independence India.
2. Examine the expansion of formal education systems after independence and analyse the challenges related to quality and regional disparities.
3. Explain the role of education in promoting equity, access, and social justice, with reference to marginalized communities.

4. Analyse how post-independence educational reforms attempted to balance cultural heritage with scientific and technological advancement.

5. Evaluate the impact of reservation and scholarship policies on social mobility and educational outcomes.

6. Critically assess why deeper structural reforms are necessary to ensure meaningful learning beyond enrolment figures.

5

The National Education Policy and Structural Transformation

5.1 Philosophical Shift Toward Learner-Centric Education

Recent education policies reflect a move away from rigid, content-heavy instruction toward learner-centric and competency-based education. Emphasis is placed on conceptual understanding, critical thinking, creativity, and problem-solving.

The philosophical foundation of contemporary education has undergone a significant transformation, moving away from teacher-dominated, content-driven instruction toward a learner-centric approach. Earlier models of education largely treated learners as passive recipients of information, where success was measured by memorization and reproduction of prescribed content. In contrast, modern educational thinking recognizes learners as active agents who construct knowledge through engagement, reflection, and interaction with their environment. This shift aligns education with the developmental needs, interests, and abilities of individual learners rather than enforcing uniform learning pathways.

Learner-centric education emphasizes conceptual clarity over rote coverage of syllabi. Instead of prioritizing the quantity of content delivered, educators focus on how deeply learners understand ideas and how effectively they can apply knowledge to real-world situations. Skills such as critical thinking, creativity, communication, and problem-solving are placed at the core of the learning process. This approach encourages questioning, exploration, and independent reasoning, enabling learners to connect classroom knowledge with everyday life and societal challenges.

Another important dimension of this philosophical shift is the move toward competency-based learning. Competencies integrate knowledge, skills, values, and attitudes, ensuring holistic development rather than narrow academic achievement. Assessment practices are also reoriented to evaluate understanding, application, and growth instead of mere factual recall. As a result, learning becomes a continuous, reflective process that values progress and mastery over competition and examination pressure.

5.2 Curriculum Flexibility and Multidisciplinary Learning

The policy framework promotes flexible curricula that allow students to explore multiple disciplines. Breaking rigid subject boundaries encourages holistic learning and adaptability. By integrating arts, sciences, and vocational skills, education becomes more relevant to real-world contexts and diverse career pathways.

Curriculum flexibility represents a deliberate shift away from rigid, compartmentalized subject structures toward a more integrated and adaptive learning framework. Traditional education systems often separated knowledge into isolated disciplines, limiting students' ability to see connections between ideas or apply learning beyond specific subjects. In contrast, a flexible curriculum allows learners to choose from a range of subjects and learning pathways, enabling them to align education with their interests, strengths, and future aspirations.

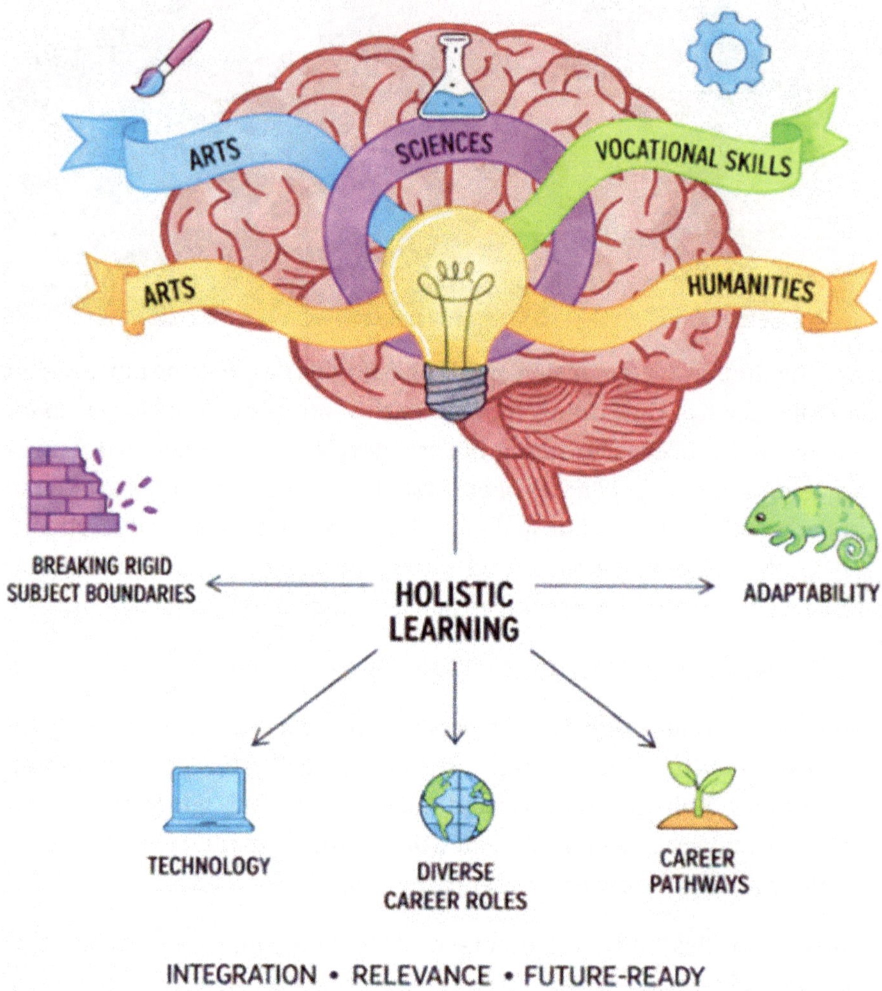

Multidisciplinary learning plays a central role in this transformation. By breaking down strict subject boundaries, students are encouraged to understand concepts from multiple perspectives. For example, a single theme such as sustainability may draw upon science to understand environmental impact, economics to analyse resource use, social studies to examine policy implications, and the arts to communicate ideas creatively. This integrated approach reflects how real-world problems function, as they rarely belong to one discipline alone.

Another important aspect of curriculum flexibility is the inclusion of arts, sports, and vocational education alongside academic subjects. When learners engage with creative arts, technical skills, and practical training, education becomes more balanced and inclusive. Such exposure helps students discover diverse talents and career possibilities while developing transferable skills like collaboration, innovation, and adaptability. It also challenges the traditional hierarchy that values academic subjects over skill-based or creative domains.

Overall, curriculum flexibility and multidisciplinary learning prepare students for a rapidly changing world where adaptability and cross-domain thinking are essential. By allowing exploration across disciplines and emphasizing meaningful connections between knowledge areas, education becomes more relevant, engaging, and responsive to individual and societal needs.

5.3 Assessment Reforms and Skill Development

Traditional rote-based examinations are gradually being replaced with continuous and formative assessments. The focus is on evaluating understanding, application, and skills rather than memorization. Assessment practices in education are undergoing a fundamental transformation, shifting away from high-stakes, rote-based examinations toward more continuous and formative methods of evaluation. Traditional exams largely emphasized memorization and the ability to reproduce information within limited timeframes. Such approaches often failed to capture a learner's true understanding, creativity, or problem-solving capacity. Contemporary assessment reforms aim to address these limitations by focusing on how students learn, apply knowledge, and develop skills over time.

Continuous and formative assessments are designed to support learning rather than merely judge performance. Regular quizzes, classroom discussions, project work, portfolios, presentations, and peer assessments provide ongoing feedback to both learners and teachers. This feedback helps identify learning gaps early and allows for timely support and improvement. Instead of viewing assessment as an endpoint, it becomes an integral part of the learning process, encouraging reflection, self-assessment, and growth.

A key feature of these reforms is the emphasis on evaluating higher-order skills such as critical thinking, analytical reasoning, communication, and collaboration. Learners are assessed on their ability to apply concepts in new situations, solve real-world problems, and demonstrate practical understanding. This approach reduces exam-related stress and promotes deeper engagement with subject matter, as success depends on comprehension and application rather than short-term memorization.

Alongside assessment reform, skill development has been integrated into mainstream education. Vocational skills, life skills, digital literacy, and interpersonal abilities are increasingly recognized as essential for employability and everyday life. By embedding these skills within academic learning, education becomes more relevant to workplace demands and social realities. Overall, assessment reforms and skill-focused education work together to produce confident, competent learners who are better prepared for professional responsibilities and lifelong learning.

Case Study: Assessment Reform and Skill Development in a Secondary School

A government secondary school implementing competency-based assessment provides a clear illustration of assessment reforms in practice.

Instead of relying solely on year-end written examinations, the school adopted a **continuous and formative assessment** model across grades.

In science classes, students were assessed through experiments, project reports, and oral explanations rather than memorized definitions. For example, while studying electricity, students designed simple circuits using low-cost materials and explained how current flows, demonstrating conceptual understanding and practical application. Teachers maintained portfolios documenting each student's progress, strengths, and areas needing improvement.

To integrate skill development, the school introduced **vocational modules** such as basic computer applications, financial literacy, and communication skills. Students learned spreadsheet usage by tracking household expenses, practiced presentation skills through group seminars, and developed teamwork through collaborative assignments. Assessment criteria included problem-solving ability, clarity of expression, and practical competence alongside subject knowledge.

Feedback was provided regularly through rubrics and one-on-one discussions, enabling students to improve continuously rather than preparing only for final exams. Over time, students showed increased confidence, reduced exam anxiety, and improved readiness for higher education and employment.

This case study demonstrates how **assessment reforms combined with skill development** shift the focus from memorization to meaningful learning, helping students acquire practical abilities and adaptable competencies required in real-world contexts.

5.4 Institutional Autonomy and Governance Reforms

Educational institutions are encouraged to adopt greater autonomy in academic and administrative matters. Governance reforms aim to improve accountability, transparency, and innovation. This

decentralization supports institutional diversity while aligning education with national development goals.

Institutional autonomy and governance reforms represent a strategic shift in how educational institutions are managed and regulated. Traditionally, many institutions operated under highly centralized control, with limited freedom to design curricula, introduce new programs, or make administrative decisions. Such rigidity often restricted innovation and responsiveness to local needs. Contemporary education reforms encourage institutions to exercise greater academic, administrative, and financial autonomy, enabling them to function more dynamically and responsibly.

Academic autonomy allows institutions to design curricula, introduce interdisciplinary courses, adopt innovative teaching methods, and update syllabi in response to emerging knowledge and societal demands. This flexibility helps institutions tailor learning experiences to student needs, regional contexts, and industry requirements. Administrative autonomy further enables efficient decision-making in areas such as faculty recruitment, infrastructure development, and student support systems, reducing delays associated with centralized approvals.

Governance reforms complement autonomy by strengthening accountability and transparency. Clear performance benchmarks, outcome-based evaluations, and participatory governance structures ensure that autonomy is exercised responsibly. Leadership bodies are expected to follow ethical practices, maintain financial discipline, and involve stakeholders such as faculty, students, and the community in decision-making. This balance between freedom and accountability fosters trust and institutional credibility.

Overall, decentralization supports institutional diversity while maintaining alignment with broader national development goals. Autonomous institutions can innovate and specialize, contributing to skill development, research, and social advancement. At the same time, governance reforms ensure that educational institutions remain committed to quality, inclusivity, and public responsibility, positioning education as a key driver of sustainable national progress.

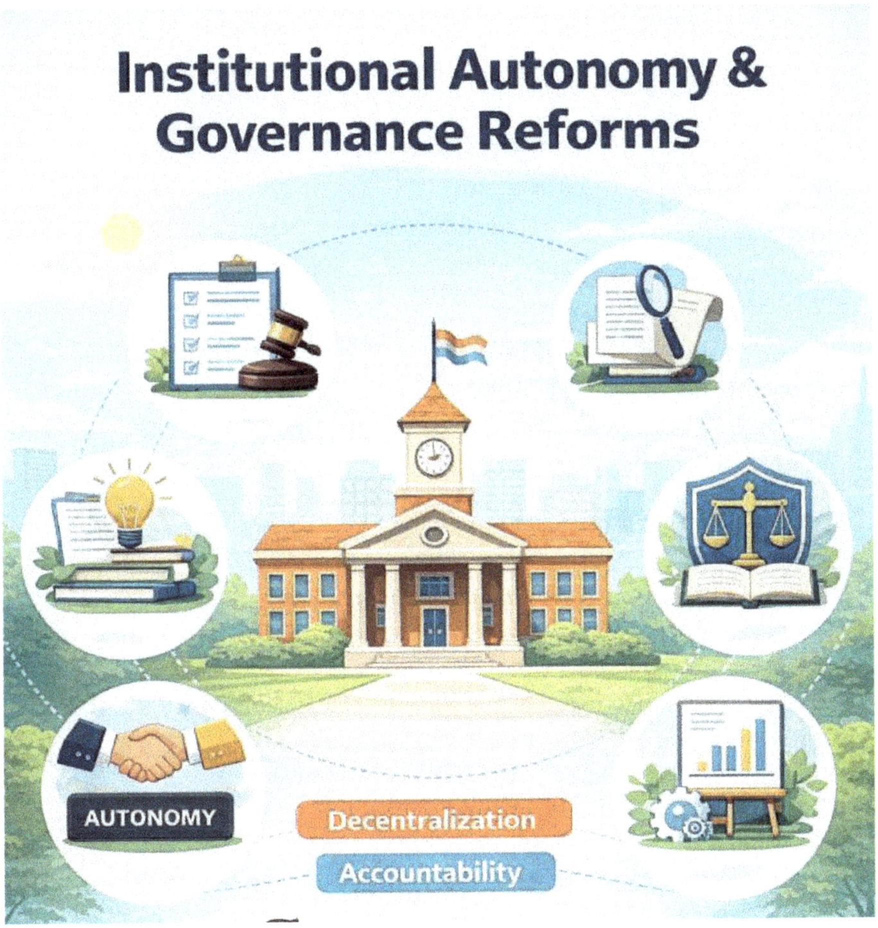

Aspect	Traditional Centralized System	Reformed Autonomous System
Academic decision-making	Curriculum and syllabi fixed by central authorities	Institutions design and update curricula based on needs
Administrative control	Limited authority over staffing and resources	Greater freedom in recruitment and resource management
Governance structure	Hierarchical and bureaucratic	Participatory and transparent governance
Accountability mechanisms	Compliance-focused inspections	Outcome-based evaluation and performance review
Innovation capacity	Restricted due to rigid regulations	Encouraged through autonomy and flexibility
Alignment with national goals	Uniform implementation	Diverse institutional approaches within national framework

Multiple Choice Questions (MCQs)

1. What is the primary focus of the National Education Policy's shift toward learner-centric education?

a) Increasing syllabus content
b) Emphasizing rote memorization
c) Promoting active participation and conceptual understanding
d) Reducing teacher involvement

Answer: c) Promoting active participation and conceptual understanding

2. Curriculum flexibility under the National Education Policy mainly aims to:

a) Eliminate all core subjects
b) Encourage specialization from early schooling
c) Allow exploration across multiple disciplines
d) Standardize education across all institutions

Answer: c) Allow exploration across multiple disciplines

3. Which assessment approach is promoted by recent education reforms?

a) Annual high-stakes examinations
b) Rote-based written tests
c) Continuous and formative assessment
d) Memorization-focused evaluations

Answer: c) Continuous and formative assessment

4. Integration of vocational and life skills into mainstream education primarily helps in:

a) Reducing academic workload
b) Enhancing employability and practical competence
c) Replacing higher education
d) Limiting career options

Answer: b) Enhancing employability and practical competence

5. Institutional autonomy in the National Education Policy is intended to:

a) Remove accountability from institutions
b) Centralize governance further
c) Promote innovation with transparency and accountability
d) Focus only on administrative independence

Answer: c) Promote innovation with transparency and accountability

Short Answer Questions

1. What is meant by learner-centric education in the context of the National Education Policy?
2. How does curriculum flexibility support multidisciplinary learning?
3. Define formative assessment and explain its role in modern education.
4. Why is skill development integrated into mainstream education under the National Education Policy?
5. What is institutional autonomy in education?
6. How do governance reforms improve accountability in educational institutions?

Long Answer Questions

1. Explain the philosophical shift from content-heavy instruction to learner-centric education introduced by the National Education Policy.
2. Discuss the importance of curriculum flexibility and multidisciplinary learning in preparing students for real-world challenges.
3. Examine the need for assessment reforms and explain how continuous and formative assessments improve learning outcomes.
4. Analyse the role of vocational and life skills in enhancing employability and holistic development under the National Education Policy.
5. Describe the significance of institutional autonomy and governance reforms in improving the quality of higher education.
6. Critically evaluate how decentralization in educational governance supports innovation while aligning institutions with national development goals.

6
Technology-Driven Learning and Digital Innovation

6.1 Digital Transformation of Teaching and Learning

Technology has transformed how education is delivered and accessed. Online platforms, virtual classrooms, and digital resources have expanded learning beyond physical boundaries.

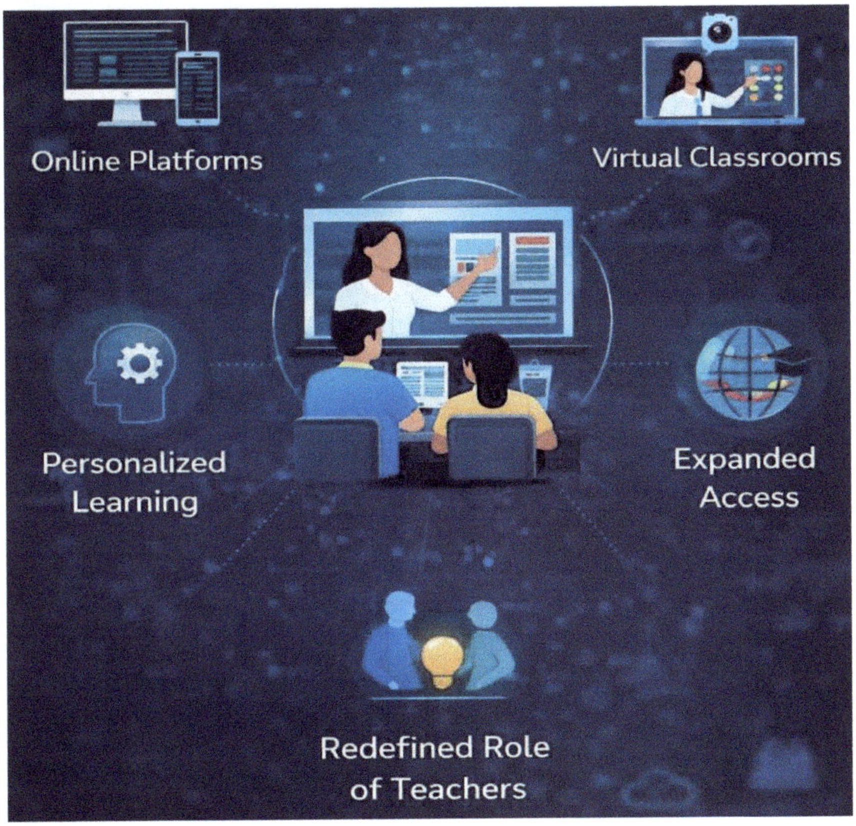

Digital transformation has fundamentally reshaped teaching and learning by moving education beyond the limits of physical classrooms. Technology now enables learning to occur anytime and anywhere through online platforms, virtual classrooms, and cloud-based educational resources. This shift has changed education from a location-bound activity into a flexible, networked experience where learners can access knowledge using computers, tablets, or smartphones.

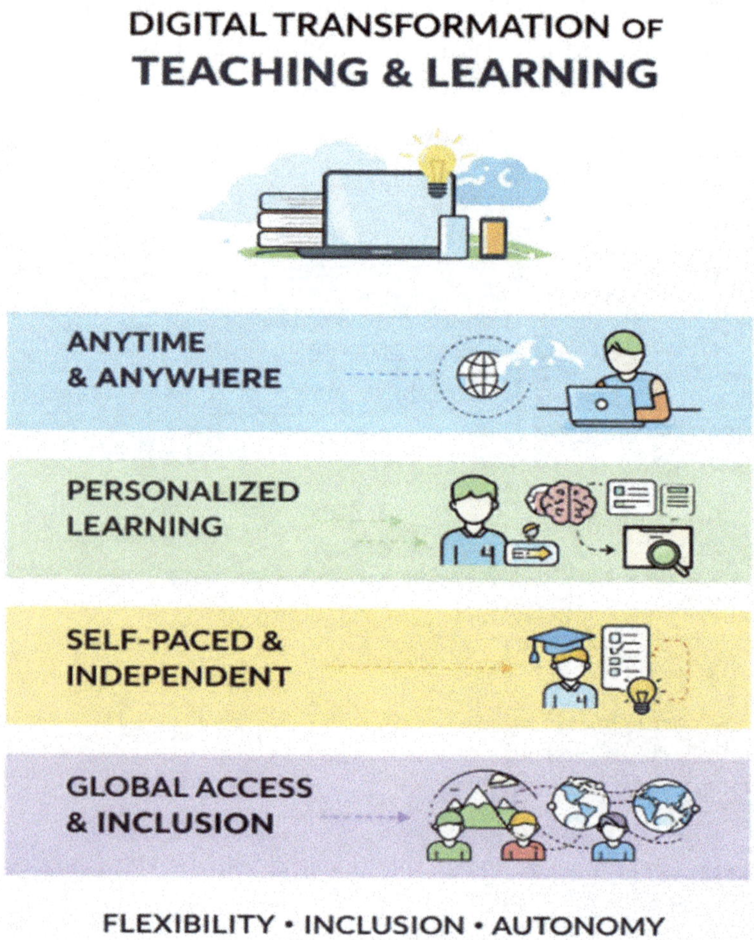

One of the most significant impacts of digital transformation is **personalized learning**. Digital tools allow educational content to adapt to individual learners' pace, interests, and abilities. Students can revisit recorded lectures, explore supplementary materials, or advance more quickly through topics they understand well. This learner-driven approach respects individual differences and supports deeper conceptual understanding rather than uniform, one-speed instruction.

Technology has also strengthened **self-paced and independent learning**. Learners are no longer entirely dependent on real-time classroom instruction. Online modules, interactive simulations, and digital assessments allow students to take greater responsibility for their learning. This encourages autonomy, time-management skills, and lifelong learning habits-competencies that are essential in a rapidly changing knowledge economy.

Another important dimension is **expanded access and inclusion**. Digital education platforms help bridge geographical and institutional barriers by making high-quality learning resources available to students in remote or underserved areas. Learners who previously faced limitations due to location, mobility, or institutional constraints can now participate in global learning environments, interact with diverse perspectives, and access expert knowledge.

Finally, digital transformation has redefined the **role of teachers**. Educators increasingly act as facilitators, mentors, and learning designers rather than sole transmitters of information. Technology supports collaborative learning, real-time feedback, and data-driven insights into student progress, enabling more informed instructional decisions.

Overall, the digital transformation of teaching and learning represents a shift toward flexibility, inclusivity, and learner empowerment. When thoughtfully integrated, technology enhances educational quality by aligning learning processes with the needs of modern learners and the demands of a digital society.

6.2 Role of Digital Platforms and Open Resources

Open educational resources and digital platforms democratize access to knowledge. Learners from diverse backgrounds can access lectures, materials, and assessments remotely.

Digital platforms and open educational resources (OER) play a transformative role in reshaping access to knowledge by removing traditional barriers associated with cost, location, and institutional affiliation. These platforms provide freely available or low-cost learning materials such as lectures, readings, videos, simulations, and assessments, allowing learners to engage with high-quality educational content regardless of their socio-economic background.

One of the most important contributions of digital platforms is the **democratization of knowledge** . In the past, access to expert instruction and authoritative resources was often limited to those enrolled in formal institutions. Today, learners from rural areas, working professionals, and non-traditional students can access the same learning materials as those in elite academic settings. This shift promotes educational equity and helps reduce disparities between privileged and underserved communities.

Open resources also strongly support **lifelong learning** . As careers evolve and knowledge rapidly becomes outdated, individuals increasingly need continuous learning opportunities. Digital platforms enable learners to update skills, explore new disciplines, or pursue personal interests at any stage of life. Learning is no longer confined to a specific age or degree program but becomes an ongoing, self-directed process.

Another key impact is the **reduced dependency on traditional institutional structures** . While universities and schools remain important, learners now have alternative pathways to knowledge acquisition. Independent learners can curate their own learning journeys using open resources, certifications, and peer learning communities. This flexibility empowers individuals to take control of their educational goals and progress at their own pace.

Finally, digital platforms encourage **inclusivity and collaboration** . Many platforms support discussion forums, peer feedback, and global learning communities where learners from different cultures and backgrounds interact. Such environments enrich understanding, promote cross-cultural exchange, and foster a sense of shared learning beyond physical classrooms.

In essence, digital platforms and open educational resources expand the reach of education, support continuous skill development, and promote inclusive learning ecosystems. By making knowledge more accessible and adaptable, they redefine education as a shared global resource rather than a limited institutional privilege.

Example: Role of Digital Platforms and Open Resources

A clear example of the role of digital platforms and open resources can be seen in a student living in a remote rural area who lacks access to well-equipped colleges or experienced teachers. Through open digital learning platforms, the student can attend recorded lectures, access freely available textbooks, attempt online quizzes, and participate in discussion forums-all using a basic internet connection and a smartphone or laptop.

For instance, a learner preparing for competitive exams or skill-based employment can study subjects such as mathematics, computer programming, or communication skills using open educational resources. These materials allow the learner to pause, rewind, and revisit concepts multiple times, enabling self-paced understanding. Peer discussion boards and online assessments further help clarify doubts without physical classroom interaction.

This example highlights how digital platforms reduce dependence on traditional institutions, expand access to quality education, and support lifelong learning. Knowledge becomes available based on motivation and effort rather than location, financial capacity, or institutional enrolment, making education more inclusive and learner driven.

6.3 Challenges of the Digital Divide

Despite technological progress, unequal access to devices, internet connectivity, and digital literacy remains a major concern. Rural and economically disadvantaged learners often face barriers to digital learning. Addressing this divide is essential to ensure that technological innovation does not widen existing educational inequalities.

The digital divide refers to the gap between individuals and communities that have adequate access to digital technologies and those that do not. Despite rapid technological advancement in education, this divide remains a serious challenge, particularly in rural regions and among economically disadvantaged groups. Access to digital learning is not determined solely by the availability of online platforms, but also by reliable internet connectivity, suitable devices, and the skills required to use them effectively.

One major challenge is **unequal access to infrastructure** . Many learners lack stable internet connections or depend on shared or low-quality devices, making sustained online learning difficult. In remote or underdeveloped areas, connectivity may be slow, expensive, or unreliable, limiting participation in virtual classes, assessments, and interactive learning activities. As a result, students in these contexts may fall behind their peers who enjoy uninterrupted digital access.

Another critical issue is **digital literacy** . Even when devices and internet access are available, learners and sometimes teachers may lack the skills needed to navigate digital platforms confidently. Limited familiarity with online tools, learning management systems, or digital communication can reduce the effectiveness of technology-based education. This skills gap can discourage learners, lower engagement, and widen learning disparities.

The digital divide also has **social and economic implications** . Students from affluent backgrounds are more likely to benefit from personalized learning tools, online tutoring, and global educational resources, while disadvantaged learners may struggle to access even basic digital content. If unaddressed, this imbalance risks reinforcing existing inequalities rather than reducing them.

Addressing the digital divide is therefore essential for inclusive educational development. Efforts such as expanding internet infrastructure, providing affordable devices, offering digital skills training, and designing low-bandwidth learning solutions are crucial. Without these measures, technological innovation in education may unintentionally widen educational inequalities instead of serving as a tool for equal opportunity and social progress.

6.4 Future Pedagogies in a Technology-Enabled Classroom

Technology is reshaping pedagogy by enabling interactive, data-driven, and adaptive learning environments. Teachers increasingly act as facilitators and mentors rather than sole knowledge providers. The future classroom blends human guidance with technological tools, emphasizing collaboration, creativity, and critical engagement.

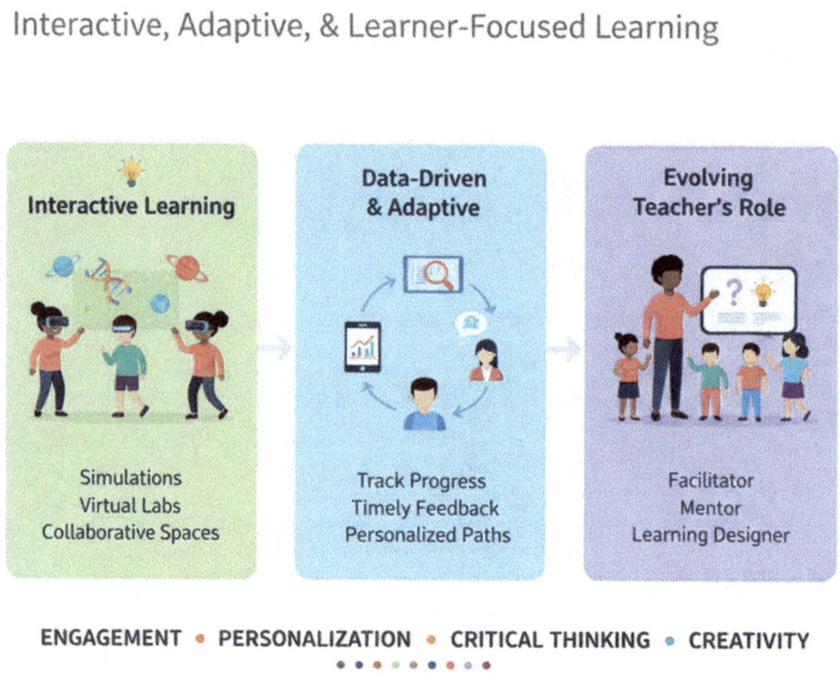

Future pedagogies in technology-enabled classrooms represent a shift from traditional, teacher-centred instruction toward more **interactive, adaptive, and learner-focused approaches** . Technology no longer serves merely as a support tool; instead, it actively shapes how learning is designed, delivered, and experienced. Digital platforms, learning analytics, and intelligent tools enable classrooms to respond dynamically to learners' needs, making education more responsive and meaningful.

One defining feature of future pedagogy is **interactive learning** . Technology allows students to engage with content through simulations, multimedia resources, virtual labs, and collaborative digital spaces. Rather than passively listening to lectures, learners actively explore concepts, test ideas, and apply knowledge in real or simulated contexts. This engagement strengthens understanding and encourages curiosity-driven learning.

Another important aspect is **data-driven and adaptive instruction** . Digital tools can track learner progress, identify gaps in understanding, and provide timely feedback. Teachers can use this information to personalize instruction, offer targeted support, or redesign learning activities. Such adaptability ensures that learners receive guidance aligned with their individual learning paths rather than a one-size-fits-all approach.

In this evolving environment, the **role of the teacher transforms significantly**. Educators increasingly function as facilitators, mentors, and learning designers. They guide discussions, support critical inquiry, encourage reflection, and help students make sense of information. Technology handles routine content delivery, allowing teachers to focus on higher-order skills such as reasoning, ethical thinking, creativity, and collaboration.

Future classrooms also emphasize **collaboration and critical engagement** . Digital tools connect learners with peers, experts, and communities beyond the classroom, fostering teamwork and shared problem-solving. Students learn to evaluate information critically, create original ideas, and communicate effectively-skills essential for participation in a knowledge-based and technologically advanced society.

Multiple Choice Questions (MCQs)

1. What is the primary impact of digital technology on teaching and learning?

A. Increased focus on rote memorization
B. Restriction of learning to classrooms
C. Expansion of flexible and personalized learning
D. Elimination of teacher involvement

Answer: C. Expansion of flexible and personalized learning

2. Which of the following best describes the role of open educational resources (OER)?

A. Limiting access to institutional learners only
B. Increasing the cost of educational materials
C. Democratizing access to knowledge
D. Replacing formal education completely

Answer: C. Democratizing access to knowledge

3. The term "digital divide" refers to:

A. Differences in teaching styles
B. The gap between traditional and modern education
C. Unequal access to digital tools and skills
D. Competition among online platforms

Answer: C. Unequal access to digital tools and skills

4. In a technology-enabled classroom, teachers primarily act as:

A. Sole transmitters of information
B. Content examiners only
C. Facilitators and mentors
D. Technical support staff

Answer: C. Facilitators and mentors

5. Which learning approach is most strongly supported by digital platforms?

A. Uniform, time-bound learning
B. Passive listening-based learning
C. Self-paced and lifelong learning
D. Memorization-focused learning

Answer: C. Self-paced and lifelong learning

Short Answer Questions

1. What is meant by technology-driven learning?
2. How do digital platforms support personalized learning?
3. Define open educational resources (OER).
4. What is the digital divide in education?
5. How has the role of teachers changed in technology-enabled classrooms?
6. Why is digital literacy important for effective online learning?

Long Answer Questions

1. Explain how digital transformation has expanded access to education beyond physical classrooms.
2. Discuss the role of digital platforms and open resources in promoting inclusive and lifelong learning.
3. Analyse the challenges posed by the digital divide and suggest measures to address them.
4. Describe future pedagogical approaches in technology-enabled classrooms and their impact on learners.
5. Examine how technology reshapes the teaching–learning process and student engagement.

7

Teacher Education, Pedagogy, and Professional Development

7.1 Evolving Role of the Teacher in Modern Indian Education

The role of teachers in India has shifted from being sole transmitters of knowledge to facilitators of learning and mentors for holistic development. Modern classrooms require teachers to encourage inquiry, dialogue, and independent thinking rather than rote memorization.

The role of the teacher in modern Indian education has undergone a significant transformation in response to changing societal needs, educational reforms, and advances in pedagogy. Traditionally, teachers were viewed as the primary authority in the classroom, responsible for delivering fixed content that students were expected to memorize and reproduce in examinations. Contemporary education, however, emphasizes understanding, application, and critical engagement, which has redefined the teacher's function.

In today's classrooms, teachers act more as facilitators and learning guides than as sole sources of information. Their responsibility is to create an environment that stimulates curiosity, encourages questioning, and supports independent thinking. Rather than focusing only on completing syllabi, teachers help learners explore concepts, connect ideas across disciplines, and relate classroom learning to real-life contexts. This shift recognizes students as active participants in their own learning journey.

Teachers also play an important mentoring role in students' holistic development. Beyond academic instruction, they support emotional well-being, ethical awareness, communication skills, and social responsibility. By fostering dialogue and inclusivity, teachers help students develop confidence, empathy, and collaboration skills essential for life beyond school. Assessment practices, too, are evolving, with teachers guiding students through reflective learning, peer interaction, and constructive feedback instead of relying solely on rote-based testing.

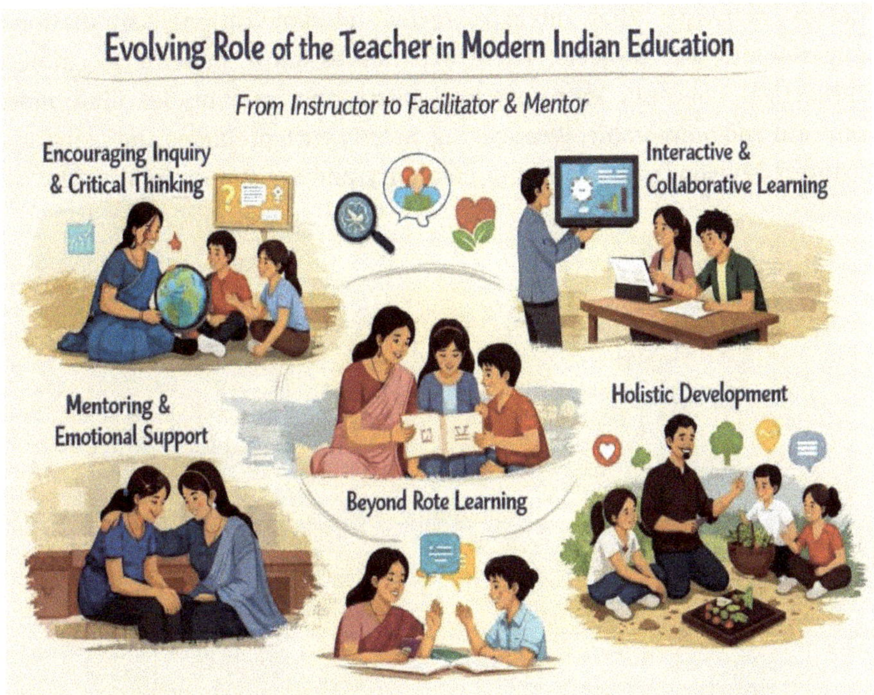

7.2 Innovations in Pedagogy and Classroom Practices

Contemporary pedagogy emphasizes experiential learning, collaborative tasks, and reflective thinking. Methods such as problem-based learning, flipped classrooms, and inquiry-driven instruction help students connect theory with practice.

Pedagogical practices in contemporary education have evolved to move beyond passive transmission of information toward active, meaningful learning experiences. Modern pedagogy emphasizes *learning by doing*, social interaction, and reflection, recognizing that students learn more effectively when they are actively engaged in constructing knowledge rather than merely receiving it. This shift reflects a deeper understanding of how learners process information, develop skills, and retain concepts over time.

Experiential learning has become a central feature of innovative classroom practices. Instead of limiting learning to textbooks and lectures, teachers design activities that involve real-world applications, simulations, experiments, and projects. These experiences allow students to connect theoretical concepts with practical situations, making learning more relevant and memorable. By engaging directly with problems and scenarios, learners develop critical thinking, creativity, and decision-making skills.

Collaborative learning is another key innovation. Group discussions, peer learning, and team-based projects encourage students to exchange ideas, negotiate meaning, and learn from diverse perspectives. Such practices help students build communication and interpersonal skills while deepening conceptual understanding. Learning becomes a shared process rather than an isolated activity, fostering a sense of responsibility and collective inquiry within the classroom.

Reflective thinking further strengthens these pedagogical approaches. Students are encouraged to reflect on what they have learned, how they learned it, and how their understanding has changed. Reflection helps learners identify gaps in knowledge, evaluate strategies, and develop metacognitive awareness, which is essential for lifelong learning.

Case Illustration:
In schools that adopt the flipped classroom model, traditional teaching structures are reversed. Students are assigned recorded video lectures or digital learning materials to study at home at their own pace. Classroom time is then devoted to discussions, problem-solving exercises, and application-based activities under the guidance of the teacher. This approach allows students to clarify doubts, apply concepts collaboratively, and receive immediate feedback. As a result, learners demonstrate higher engagement, improved conceptual clarity, and greater confidence in applying knowledge, while teachers can focus on supporting deeper understanding rather than repetitive lecturing.

7.3 Teacher Training and Continuous Professional Development

Effective education reform depends on well-trained teachers who continuously update their skills. Modern teacher education focuses on pedagogical skills, assessment literacy, technology integration, and inclusive practices.

Sustainable improvement in the quality of education is closely linked to the preparation and ongoing development of teachers. In a rapidly changing educational landscape, initial teacher training alone is no longer sufficient. Effective education reform depends on teachers who continually update their knowledge, refine their teaching practices, and respond to new curricular goals, learner needs, and technological advancements.

Modern teacher education places strong emphasis on pedagogical competence rather than only subject expertise. Teachers are trained to design learner-centred lessons, use varied instructional strategies, and apply assessment methods that evaluate understanding rather than memorization. Assessment literacy has become particularly important, enabling teachers to use formative assessments, feedback mechanisms, and reflective evaluation to support student growth. This approach helps teachers identify learning gaps early and adjust instruction accordingly.

Technology integration is another core component of contemporary teacher training. Digital tools, online platforms, and multimedia resources have become integral to teaching and learning processes. Teacher development programs now focus on helping educators use technology meaningfully-to enhance engagement, personalize learning, and support collaboration-rather than treating it as an add-on. Alongside this, inclusive education practices are emphasized to ensure that teachers can effectively address the diverse needs of learners, including students with different abilities, learning styles, and socio-cultural backgrounds.

Continuous professional development (CPD) provides a structured way for teachers to adapt to evolving educational demands. Through workshops, seminars, peer-learning communities, and reflective practice, teachers remain informed about new teaching methods, policy changes, and classroom innovations. CPD also promotes professional confidence and motivation, reinforcing teaching as a dynamic and evolving profession.

7.4 Teacher Motivation, Ethics, and Educational Leadership

Teachers play a critical role in shaping values, ethics, and social responsibility. Motivation, professional integrity, and leadership skills are essential for creating positive learning environments. Teachers who act as role models foster trust, discipline, and inspiration among students.

Teachers occupy a central position in the moral and social development of learners, extending their influence far beyond academic instruction. In modern education, teachers are not only facilitators of knowledge but also shapers of values, attitudes, and civic responsibility. Their motivation, ethical conduct, and leadership abilities directly affect the quality of the learning environment and the overall culture of educational institutions.

Teacher motivation is a key driver of effective teaching and sustained commitment. Motivated teachers display enthusiasm, creativity, and resilience, which positively influences student engagement and learning outcomes. When teachers feel valued, supported, and professionally fulfilled, they are more likely to invest effort in innovative practices and individualized student support. Motivation is strengthened through recognition, opportunities for growth, and a sense of purpose in contributing to societal development through education.

Ethical conduct and professional integrity form the foundation of trust between teachers and learners. Teachers model honesty, fairness, respect, and responsibility through their daily interactions. By maintaining ethical standards in assessment, discipline, and relationships, teachers create safe and inclusive learning spaces where students feel respected and encouraged to express themselves. Such environments nurture discipline not through fear, but through mutual respect and shared values.

Educational leadership further enhances the teacher's role in shaping institutions and communities. Teachers who demonstrate leadership take initiative, collaborate with colleagues, and contribute to decision-making processes. Leadership in education is not limited to administrative positions; it emerges through mentoring, curriculum development, innovation, and community engagement. Teacher leaders help bridge gaps between policy and classroom practice, ensuring that educational goals are meaningfully implemented.

Multiple Choice Questions (MCQs)

1. In modern Indian education, the primary role of a teacher has shifted toward:

a) Delivering fixed content for examinations
b) Enforcing strict discipline and memorization
c) Facilitating learning and mentoring holistic development
d) Limiting classroom interaction

Answer: c) Facilitating learning and mentoring holistic development

2. Which pedagogical approach emphasizes real-world problem solving and active student participation?

a) Rote learning
b) Lecture-based instruction
c) Problem-based learning
d) Examination-oriented teaching

Answer: c) Problem-based learning

3. The flipped classroom model primarily aims to:

a) Replace teachers with digital tools
b) Shift lectures to home and use class time for application
c) Reduce classroom interaction
d) Eliminate assessments

Answer: b) Shift lectures to home and use class time for application

4. Continuous professional development (CPD) for teachers mainly helps in:

a) Completing the syllabus faster
b) Maintaining traditional teaching methods
c) Adapting to curricular, technological, and learner diversity changes
d) Reducing teacher accountability

Answer: c) Adapting to curricular, technological, and learner diversity changes

5. Teacher leadership in schools most effectively contributes to:

a) Centralized control by administrators
b) Improved institutional culture and student outcomes
c) Increased workload without benefits
d) Limiting collaboration among teachers

Answer: b) Improved institutional culture and student outcomes

Short Answer Questions

1. How has the role of the teacher changed in modern Indian education?
2. What is meant by experiential learning in contemporary pedagogy?
3. Why is continuous professional development important for teachers?
4. What is a flipped classroom, and how does it support active learning?
5. How do ethical values of teachers influence the classroom environment?
6. In what ways can teachers act as leaders without holding administrative positions?

Long Answer Questions

1. Discuss the evolving role of teachers from knowledge transmitters to facilitators and mentors in modern education.
2. Explain innovative pedagogical practices such as problem-based learning and collaborative learning, highlighting their impact on student engagement.
3. Analyse the significance of teacher training and continuous professional development in improving educational quality.
4. Describe the role of technology integration in modern pedagogy and teacher education.
5. Examine the importance of teacher motivation and professional ethics in shaping students' values and social responsibility.

6. Evaluate how teacher leadership contributes to institutional development and improved student learning outcomes.

8

Inclusivity, Equity, and Multilingual Education

8.1 Education for Social Inclusion and Marginalized Communities

Inclusive education aims to provide equal learning opportunities for students from disadvantaged backgrounds, including economically weaker sections, rural populations, and historically marginalized communities. Policies focus on removing barriers related to access, affordability, and discrimination.

Education for social inclusion is rooted in the principle that learning should be accessible, equitable, and empowering for all sections of society, regardless of socio-economic status, geography, gender, caste, or cultural background. In the Indian context, inclusive education has emerged as a crucial strategy to address long-standing inequalities faced by economically weaker sections, rural learners, tribal populations, and historically marginalized communities. The core objective is not merely enrolment, but meaningful participation and success within the education system.

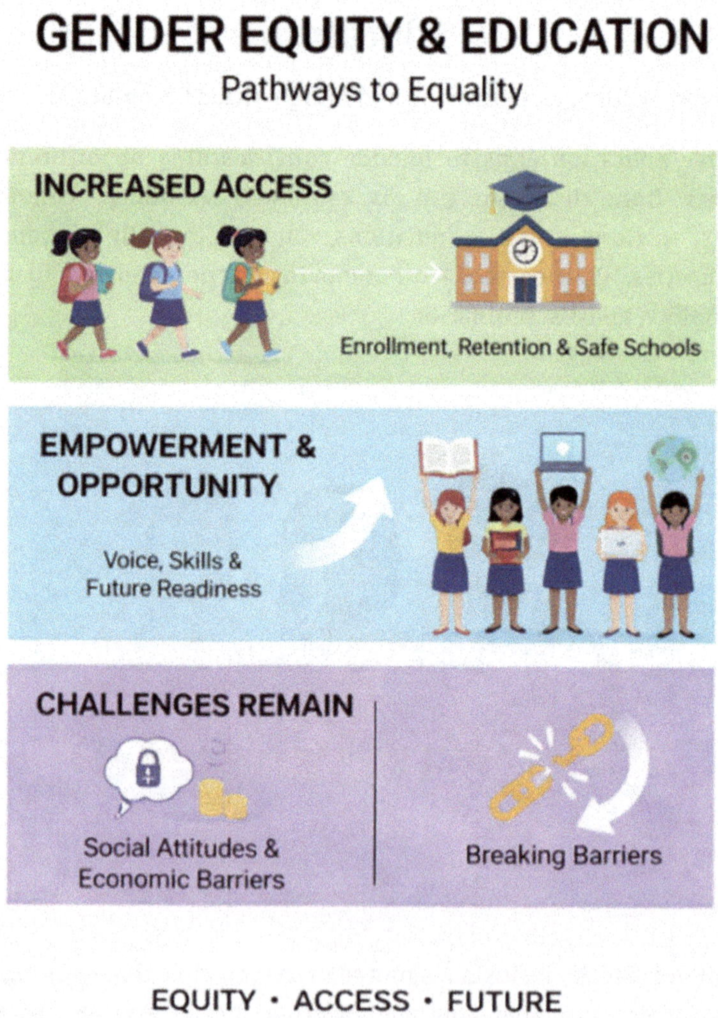

Inclusive education policies emphasize the removal of structural and social barriers that prevent equal access to learning. These barriers often include poverty, lack of nearby schools, language disadvantages, social discrimination, early entry into labour, and limited exposure to supportive learning environments. To address these challenges, governments and institutions adopt multi-layered interventions such as financial assistance, infrastructure development, mid-day meal schemes, free textbooks, digital access initiatives, and community-based awareness programs. Such measures aim to ensure that students are not excluded due to circumstances beyond their control.

A critical aspect of inclusion is affordability. For many marginalized families, the cost of education extends beyond tuition to include uniforms, transportation, and learning materials. Scholarship programs, fee waivers, and conditional cash transfers reduce this financial burden and encourage sustained attendance. At the same time, inclusive education also focuses on creating safe and respectful learning spaces that challenge discrimination and promote dignity, belonging, and self-confidence among learners from disadvantaged backgrounds.

8.2 Gender Equity and Education

Education plays a transformative role in achieving gender equality. Increased female enrolment, retention initiatives, and safety-focused school environments have expanded educational access for girls. However, social attitudes and economic constraints still influence participation.

Education is one of the most powerful instruments for advancing gender equity, as it directly influences individual empowerment, social mobility, and intergenerational development. When girls and women gain access to quality education, the benefits extend beyond personal growth to improved health outcomes, economic participation, and social decision-making within families and communities. In many societies, including India, sustained efforts have been made to reduce gender disparities in education through targeted policies and programs.

Over the years, increased female enrolment has been achieved through initiatives such as free schooling, scholarships, provision of uniforms and textbooks, and incentive-based schemes for families. Retention has become an equally important focus, as enrolling girls alone does not guarantee completion of education. Programs addressing dropout causes-such as household responsibilities, early marriage, safety concerns, and lack of sanitation facilities-have significantly improved continuation rates. The creation of gender-sensitive infrastructure, including separate toilets, safe transportation, and secure school environments, has further encouraged regular attendance among girls.

Despite this progress, gender equity in education continues to be shaped by deep-rooted social attitudes and economic constraints. In some communities, education for boys is still prioritized due to traditional perceptions of gender roles, while girls are expected to contribute to domestic work or caregiving. Poverty amplifies these challenges, as families facing financial hardship may view girls' education as less immediately valuable compared to income-generating activities or early marriage. These factors highlight that gender equity is not solely an educational issue but a broader social and cultural one.

Case Illustration:

Community-based awareness programs have proven effective in addressing these barriers at the grassroots level. Such initiatives involve local leaders, parents, women's groups, and educators working together to emphasize the long-term benefits of girls' education. Through discussions, workshops, and role-model narratives, these programs challenge stereotypes and reshape attitudes toward female learning. In many rural areas, this collective engagement has resulted in higher enrolment of girls and a noticeable delay in dropout rates. Families become more supportive when they understand how education enhances girls' self-reliance, employment prospects, and overall well-being.

8.3 Multilingual and Mother-Tongue-Based Instruction

Learning in one's mother tongue enhances comprehension, cognitive development, and cultural identity, especially in early education. Multilingual education supports smoother transitions to additional languages while preserving linguistic diversity.

Mother-tongue-based instruction recognizes that children learn most effectively when education begins in the language they speak and understand at home. In the early years of schooling, language is the foundation through which concepts, values, and cognitive skills are formed. When instruction is delivered in a familiar language, learners are better able to grasp ideas, ask questions, and express their understanding. This approach reduces anxiety, prevents early learning gaps, and supports healthy cognitive and emotional development.

Beyond comprehension, mother-tongue education plays a vital role in strengthening cultural identity. Language carries traditions, social meanings, and ways of thinking that connect learners to their communities.

When schools value and use local and regional languages, children feel respected and included, which enhances motivation and self-esteem. This sense of belonging is particularly important for first-generation learners and children from linguistically marginalized backgrounds, who may otherwise feel disconnected from formal education.

Multilingual education builds on this foundation by gradually introducing additional languages-such as regional, national, or global languages-without replacing the mother tongue abruptly. Instead of forcing an early switch to an unfamiliar language, learners transition step by step, allowing cognitive skills developed in the first language to support the acquisition of new ones. Research and classroom practice show that strong literacy in the mother tongue makes it easier for students to learn second and third languages, as skills like reading comprehension, vocabulary building, and logical reasoning are transferable across languages.

Example:
In many educational settings, early-grade instruction is conducted primarily in regional or home languages, with additional languages introduced gradually through oral activities, storytelling, and basic literacy exercises. As students' progress, the use of multiple languages increases in a structured manner. This model has led to improved reading skills, stronger conceptual clarity, and greater confidence among young learners. Children participate more actively in class discussions and demonstrate a willingness to engage with new languages rather than feeling intimidated by them.

Overall, multilingual and mother-tongue-based instruction promotes inclusive, effective, and culturally responsive education. By valuing linguistic diversity while preparing learners for broader communication needs, this approach balances local relevance with global readiness, ensuring that language becomes a bridge to learning rather than a barrier.

8.4 Inclusive Education for Learners with Special Needs

Inclusive classrooms recognize diverse learning abilities and aim to accommodate students with physical, cognitive, or emotional challenges. Adapted curricula, assistive technologies, and trained educators support inclusive learning environments.
Inclusive education for learners with special needs is grounded in the belief that all children, regardless of physical, cognitive, sensory, or emotional differences, have the right to learn together in supportive and respectful environments. Rather than isolating students with disabilities, inclusive classrooms emphasize participation, accessibility, and shared learning experiences. This approach views diversity in abilities not as a limitation, but as a natural part of the learning community.

Inclusive classrooms are designed to accommodate varied learning needs through flexible teaching strategies and adapted curricula. Instruction is often differentiated, allowing concepts to be presented in multiple ways-such as visual aids, hands-on activities, simplified texts, or interactive exercises-so that learners can engage according to their strengths. This flexibility benefits not only students with special needs but also enhances learning for all students by addressing different learning styles.

Assistive technologies play a crucial role in enabling inclusion. Tools such as screen readers, speech-to-text software, hearing aids, tactile learning materials, and alternative communication devices help learners overcome specific barriers to participation. When combined with accessible classroom layouts and inclusive assessment methods, these technologies allow students with disabilities to demonstrate understanding without being constrained by conventional formats.

Equally important is the role of trained educators. Teachers equipped with knowledge of inclusive pedagogy, special education strategies, and emotional support techniques are better prepared to create welcoming classrooms. Collaboration with special educators, counsellors, and parents further strengthens individualized support, ensuring that learners receive consistent guidance both inside and outside school.

Multiple Choice Questions (MCQs)

1. What is the primary objective of inclusive education?

   a) To standardize learning outcomes for all students
   b) To provide equal learning opportunities by addressing diverse needs
   c) To separate learners based on abilities
   d) To prioritize academic competition

Answer: b) To provide equal learning opportunities by addressing diverse needs

2. Which factor most commonly limits educational access for marginalized communities?

   a) Excessive curriculum content
   b) Lack of qualified teachers only

c) Barriers related to poverty, geography, and discrimination
d) Overuse of digital technology

Answer: c) Barriers related to poverty, geography, and discrimination

3. How does education contribute to gender equity?

a) By treating boys and girls identically in all contexts
b) By focusing only on urban schooling
c) By empowering girls through access, retention, and safe learning environments
d) By reducing the role of families in education

Answer: c) By empowering girls through access, retention, and safe learning environments

4. Why is mother-tongue-based instruction especially effective in early education?

a) It eliminates the need to learn additional languages
b) It enhances comprehension and cognitive development
c) It focuses only on cultural traditions
d) It delays literacy development

Answer: b) It enhances comprehension and cognitive development

5. Which practice best supports learners with special needs in inclusive classrooms?
a) Uniform teaching methods for all students
b) Exclusive special schools only
c) Adapted curricula, assistive technologies, and trained educators
d) Limiting peer interaction

Answer: c) Adapted curricula, assistive technologies, and trained educators

Short Answer Questions

1. What is meant by inclusive education in the context of marginalized communities?

2. How do scholarship and support schemes promote educational equity?

3. State two ways education helps in achieving gender equality.

4. Why is mother-tongue-based instruction important in early childhood education?

5. What role do assistive technologies play in inclusive classrooms?

6. How do community-based programs support girls' education in rural areas?

Long Answer Questions

1. Explain the concept of social inclusion in education and discuss the major challenges faced by marginalized learners.

2. Analyse the role of education in promoting gender equity, highlighting social and economic barriers that still exist.

3. Discuss the significance of multilingual education in preserving cultural identity while enhancing learning outcomes.

4. Examine how mother-tongue-based instruction supports cognitive development and smoother language transitions.

5. Describe inclusive education practices for learners with special needs, emphasizing the role of teachers and technology.

6. Evaluate how inclusive education contributes to social integration, empathy, and national development.

9

The Future of Indian Education in a Global Knowledge Economy

9.1 Globalization and Internationalization of Education

Indian education is increasingly influenced by global standards, collaborations, and mobility. International partnerships, student exchange programs, and cross-border research enhance academic exposure while raising questions about cultural balance.

Globalization has significantly reshaped the landscape of Indian education by connecting it with international academic systems, standards, and practices. Educational institutions in India are no longer confined to national boundaries; instead, they actively engage with global networks of knowledge, research, and innovation. This process, often described as the internationalization of education, involves the integration of global perspectives into teaching, learning, and institutional governance while operating within a local context.

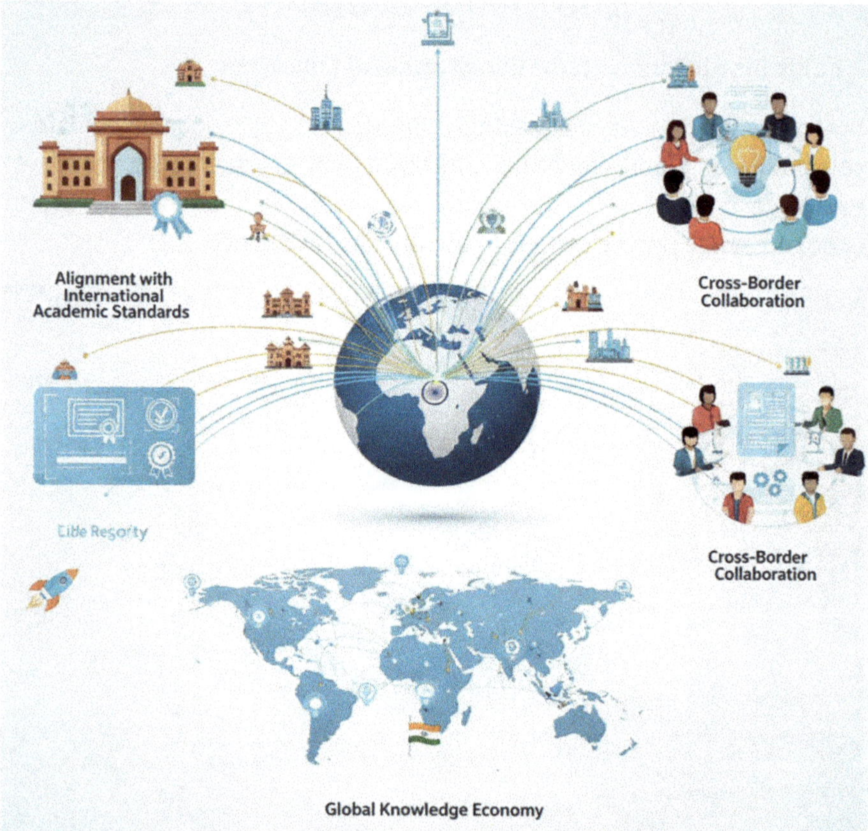

One major dimension of this shift is the alignment with international academic standards. Indian universities increasingly adopt globally recognized curricula frameworks, credit transfer systems, outcome-based education models, and quality assurance mechanisms. These changes aim to ensure that Indian degrees are comparable and competitive worldwide, thereby improving the global employability and mobility of graduates.

Exposure to international benchmarks also encourages institutions to improve pedagogy, research rigor, and assessment practices.

Another important aspect is cross-border collaboration. Partnerships between Indian and foreign universities promote joint research, faculty exchange, collaborative publications, and shared academic resources. Such collaborations expand intellectual horizons by exposing students and researchers to diverse methodologies, interdisciplinary approaches, and global problem-solving perspectives. At the same time, they enable Indian institutions to contribute indigenous knowledge, contextual insights, and regional expertise to global academic discourse.

Student mobility further strengthens internationalization. Exchange programs, study-abroad opportunities, and joint degree pathways allow learners to experience different academic cultures and social environments. These experiences help students develop intercultural competence, adaptability, and a broader worldview-skills that are increasingly essential in a globalized workforce. However, this mobility also raises important questions about accessibility, affordability, and the risk of unequal participation favouring privileged groups.

While globalization offers clear academic advantages, it also presents cultural and ethical challenges. Excessive reliance on foreign models can risk marginalizing local languages, knowledge traditions, and social priorities. Therefore, a balanced approach is essential-one that embraces global engagement while preserving cultural identity and national educational goals. Effective internationalization does not replace local relevance; instead, it integrates global exposure with contextual grounding, ensuring that education remains socially meaningful and culturally rooted even as it becomes globally connected.

9.2 Research, Innovation, and Knowledge Creation

Future education systems prioritize research, innovation, and problem-solving over information accumulation. Encouraging inquiry-based

learning and interdisciplinary research strengthens India's position in the global knowledge economy.

Contemporary and future-oriented education systems are increasingly centred on research, innovation, and the active creation of knowledge rather than the passive accumulation of information. In the Indian context, this shift reflects a growing recognition that economic growth, technological leadership, and social development depend on the ability to generate original ideas, solve complex problems, and translate knowledge into practical impact. Education is thus evolving from a content-driven model to an inquiry-driven ecosystem that nurtures curiosity, experimentation, and critical thinking.

A key feature of this transformation is the emphasis on inquiry-based learning. Students are encouraged to question assumptions, explore multiple perspectives, and engage in investigative processes rather than simply reproducing textbook knowledge. Research-oriented pedagogy promotes skills such as hypothesis formulation, data analysis, interpretation, and evidence-based reasoning. These competencies not only prepare learners for academic research but also equip them to address real-world challenges in science, technology, policy, and society.

Interdisciplinary research further strengthens innovation by breaking down traditional subject boundaries. Complex problems-such as climate change, public health, urban development, and digital transformation-cannot be addressed through single-discipline approaches. By integrating insights from engineering, social sciences, humanities, and management, Indian higher education institutions foster holistic problem-solving and creative solutions. This interdisciplinary orientation also aligns Indian research with global trends, enhancing international collaboration and academic visibility.

Innovation ecosystems within universities play a crucial role in translating research into societal and economic value. Dedicated innovation hubs, incubation centres, and research parks connect students and faculty with industry, startups, and government agencies. These platforms expose learners to real-world challenges, enabling applied research, prototype development, and entrepreneurial experimentation. Students gain hands-on experience in design thinking, commercialization, and innovation management, bridging the gap between academic research and practical application.

By prioritizing research, innovation, and knowledge creation, Indian education strengthens its contribution to the global knowledge economy. This approach not only enhances academic excellence but also supports national development by producing skilled researchers, innovators, and problem-solvers capable of driving sustainable growth and global competitiveness.

9.3 Lifelong Learning and Workforce Readiness

Rapid technological and economic change requires continuous skill development beyond formal education. Lifelong learning enables individuals to adapt to evolving career demands and social responsibilities.

Rapid technological advancement, automation, and shifting economic structures have fundamentally changed the nature of work and careers. In this context, education can no longer be viewed as a one-time phase confined to early life. Lifelong learning has emerged as a critical necessity, enabling individuals to continuously update their knowledge, skills, and competencies in response to evolving professional and societal demands. Workforce readiness today depends not only on initial qualifications but on the capacity to learn, unlearn, and relearn across the lifespan.

Lifelong learning supports adaptability in an environment where job roles frequently change and new occupations emerge. Skills that are relevant today may become obsolete within a few years due to technological disruption. Continuous learning helps individuals stay aligned with industry trends, digital tools, and emerging practices. This ongoing skill development enhances employability, reduces the risk of workforce displacement, and empowers individuals to navigate career transitions with confidence.

Another important dimension of lifelong learning is its role in bridging the gap between education and industry needs. Traditional degree programs often struggle to keep pace with rapidly changing skill requirements. Flexible learning pathways-such as short-term courses, modular programs, micro-credentials, and competency-based training-allow learners to acquire targeted skills efficiently. These models emphasize practical relevance, hands-on learning, and immediate applicability in the workplace, making education more responsive to real-world demands.

Lifelong learning also promotes inclusive workforce participation. Working professionals, caregivers, and individuals returning to the workforce benefit from learning formats that accommodate diverse schedules and responsibilities. Online platforms, blended learning models, and self-paced programs remove barriers related to time, location, and age. This inclusivity ensures that learning opportunities remain accessible throughout different stages of life, supporting both personal growth and economic productivity.

Beyond technical skills, lifelong learning nurtures broader competencies such as problem-solving, communication, ethical reasoning, and adaptability. These transferable skills are essential for navigating uncertainty and contributing meaningfully to society. By fostering a culture of continuous learning, education systems strengthen workforce readiness while empowering individuals to remain resilient, relevant, and socially engaged in an ever-changing world.

9.4 Balancing Indian Values with Global Competence

The future of Indian education lies in harmonizing cultural heritage with global competitiveness. Education must nurture ethical awareness, social responsibility, and sustainability while equipping learners with globally relevant skills.

The future direction of Indian education depends on its ability to balance deep-rooted cultural values with the demands of global competence. As learners increasingly participate in international academic, professional, and digital spaces, education must equip them with globally relevant skills while preserving ethical foundations, social sensitivity, and cultural identity. This balance ensures that progress and modernization do not come at the cost of values that have historically shaped Indian society.

Indian educational traditions have long emphasized moral development, collective well-being, respect for diversity, and harmony with nature. Concepts such as ethical conduct, social duty, and sustainability were integral to traditional learning systems. In a globalized world, these values remain highly relevant, particularly as societies face challenges related to environmental degradation, social inequality, and ethical dilemmas arising from rapid technological change. Education must therefore nurture responsible global citizens who are not only skilled but also ethically grounded.

At the same time, global competence requires learners to develop critical thinking, digital literacy, cross-cultural communication, and problem-solving abilities. Exposure to international standards, emerging technologies, and diverse perspectives enables students to function effectively in global academic and professional environments. Indian education must integrate these competencies into curricula without promoting cultural homogenization or excessive dependence on external models.

A balanced approach lies in contextual integration rather than replacement. By embedding traditional knowledge systems, local histories, indigenous sciences, and ethical philosophies alongside modern scientific and technological education, curricula can offer a holistic learning experience. This integration helps learners appreciate the relevance of cultural wisdom in addressing contemporary global challenges, such as sustainability, public health, and social cohesion.

Multiple Choice Questions (MCQs)

1. What is the primary focus of the future Indian education system in a global knowledge economy?

A. Memorization of information
B. Rigid discipline-based learning
C. Knowledge creation, innovation, and adaptability
D. Exclusive focus on national curricula

Answer: C. Knowledge creation, innovation, and adaptability

2. Which factor best represents the internationalization of Indian education?

A. Eliminating local languages from curricula
B. Adopting only foreign education models
C. Academic collaborations, student mobility, and global standards
D. Restricting education to domestic institutions

Answer: C. Academic collaborations, student mobility, and global standards

3. Why is lifelong learning essential in the future workforce?

A. To replace formal education entirely
B. To reduce the need for professional degrees
C. To help individuals adapt to technological and economic changes
D. To delay entry into the job market

Answer: C. To help individuals adapt to technological and economic changes

4. How does interdisciplinary research contribute to India's global knowledge economy?

A. By limiting research to single disciplines
B. By encouraging rote learning
C. By addressing complex problems through integrated

perspectives
D. By focusing only on theoretical knowledge

Answer: C. By addressing complex problems through integrated perspectives

5. What does balancing Indian values with global competence primarily aim to achieve?

A. Cultural isolation from the global community
B. Complete replacement of traditional knowledge
C. Ethical, socially responsible, and globally skilled learners
D. Uniform education systems across all countries

Answer: C. Ethical, socially responsible, and globally skilled learners

Short Answer Questions

1. What is meant by the globalization of Indian education?
2. Define lifelong learning in the context of workforce readiness.
3. How does interdisciplinary research support innovation in education?
4. Why is inquiry-based learning important for knowledge creation?
5. What role do international collaborations play in higher education?
6. Explain the importance of integrating Indian values into modern education.

Long Answer Questions

1. Discuss how globalization and internationalization are transforming the Indian education system.
2. Explain the role of research and innovation in strengthening India's position in the global knowledge economy.

3. Analyse the importance of lifelong learning in addressing rapid technological and economic changes.
4. Examine the need to balance Indian cultural values with global competencies in future education models.
5. Describe how university-based innovation hubs contribute to applied research and entrepreneurial thinking.
6. Evaluate the challenges and opportunities faced by Indian education in preparing globally competent and socially responsible learners.

References

Chapter 1: Foundations of Indian Education in Ancient Civilization

1. Altekar, A. S. (1965). *Education in Ancient India*. Motilal Banarsidass.
2. Sharma, R. S. (2005). *India's Ancient Past*. Oxford University Press.
3. Mukherjee, S. N. (1951). *History of Education in India*. Acharya Book Depot.

Chapter 2: Medieval Transformations and Knowledge Transmission

1. Basham, A. L. (2004). *The Wonder That Was India*. Picador.
2. Habib, I. (2008). *Economic History of Medieval India*. Pearson Education.
3. Saliba, G. (2007). *Islamic Science and the Making of the European Renaissance*. MIT Press.

Chapter 3: Colonial Influence and the Restructuring of Education

1. Macaulay, T. B. (1835). *Minute on Indian Education*. British Parliamentary Papers.
2. Nurullah, S., & Naik, J. P. (1951). *A History of Education in India during the British Period*. Macmillan.
3. Viswanathan, G. (1989). *Masks of Conquest: Literary Study and British Rule in India*. Oxford University Press.

Chapter 4: Post-Independence Educational Reforms and Nation Building

1. Government of India. (1966). *Education and National Development (Kothari Commission Report)*. Ministry of Education.
2. Government of India. (1986). *National Policy on Education*. Ministry of Human Resource Development.

3. Tilak, J. B. G. (1993). *Education and Development in India.* Gyan Publishing House.

Chapter 5: National Education Policy and Structural Transformation

1. Government of India. (2020). *National Education Policy 2020.* Ministry of Education.
2. OECD. (2018). *Education 2030: The Future of Education and Skills.* OECD Publishing.
3. National Council of Educational Research and Training (NCERT). (2021). *Curriculum Reform and Pedagogy.* NCERT.

Chapter 6: Technology-Driven Learning and Digital Innovation

1. UNESCO. (2021). *Reimagining Our Futures Together: A New Social Contract for Education.* UNESCO.
2. World Bank. (2020). *Remote Learning and COVID-19: The Use of Educational Technologies.* World Bank.
3. Selwyn, N. (2016). *Education and Technology: Key Issues and Debates.* Bloomsbury Academic.

Chapter 7: Teacher Education, Pedagogy, and Professional Development

1. National Council for Teacher Education (NCTE). (2014). *Teacher Education Regulations.* NCTE.
2. Darling-Hammond, L. (2017). *Teacher Education around the World.* Routledge.
3. Government of India. (2020). *National Professional Standards for Teachers (Draft).* Ministry of Education.

Chapter 8: Inclusivity, Equity, and Multilingual Education

1. UNESCO. (2009). *Policy Guidelines on Inclusion in Education.* UNESCO.

2. Skutnabb-Kangas, T. (2000). *Linguistic Genocide in Education*. Lawrence Erlbaum Associates.

3. Government of India. (2019). *Samagra Shiksha Framework*. Ministry of Education.

Chapter 9: The Future of Indian Education in a Global Knowledge Economy

1. World Economic Forum. (2020). *The Future of Jobs Report*. WEF.

2. Marginson, S. (2016). *Higher Education and the Common Good*. Melbourne University Press.

3. Altbach, P. G., & Knight, J. (2007). The internationalization of higher education. *Journal of Studies in International Education*, 11(3–4), 290–305.

APPENDIX

1. Glossary of Key Terms

- **Gurukul System** – An ancient Indian residential education model where students lived with the teacher and learned through experiential, value-based instruction.
- **Holistic Education** – An approach to learning that integrates intellectual, emotional, physical, ethical, and social development.
- **Multidisciplinary Education** – A learning structure that allows students to engage with multiple disciplines rather than rigid subject silos.
- **Learner-Centric Pedagogy** – Teaching methods that place students' interests, abilities, and active participation at the centre of learning.
- **Competency-Based Learning** – An educational model focused on mastery of skills and concepts rather than time-based progression.
- **Digital Divide** – Inequality in access to digital technologies, connectivity, and digital literacy.
- **Inclusive Education** – Educational practices designed to accommodate learners from diverse social, economic, linguistic, and ability backgrounds.
- **Mother-Tongue Instruction** – Teaching in a learner's first language, particularly in early education, to enhance comprehension and retention.
- **Lifelong Learning** – Continuous learning across the lifespan to adapt to personal, social, and professional change.
- **Knowledge Economy** – An economy driven by information, innovation, research, and human capital rather than physical resources alone.

2. Data Sources and Datasets

This book draws conceptually and analytically from the following **authoritative data sources**, which support policy analysis, trends, and educational outcomes:

- National education policy documents and government education reports
- Census and literacy data published by national statistical agencies
- School and higher education enrolment and retention statistics
- Reports on digital education initiatives and technology adoption
- International comparative education datasets
- Surveys on teacher education, professional development, and learning outcomes
- Research datasets related to gender equity, inclusion, and multilingual education

These sources collectively provide longitudinal, regional, and comparative perspectives on Indian education.

3. Tools and Frameworks

The following **conceptual and operational tools** underpin the discussions across chapters:

- **Policy Analysis Frameworks** – Used to examine historical and contemporary education reforms
- **Curriculum Mapping Models** – For understanding subject integration and learning progression
- **Outcome-Based Education Frameworks** – To evaluate competency and skill development

- **Digital Learning Ecosystem Models** – For analysing technology-enabled education
- **Teacher Professional Development Frameworks** – Addressing training, ethics, and leadership
- **Equity and Inclusion Models** – Assessing access, participation, and learning fairness
- **Global Benchmarking Frameworks** – Comparing Indian education with international systems

These frameworks support evidence-based analysis while maintaining contextual relevance.

4. References for Further Reading

Readers interested in deeper exploration may consult:

- Scholarly books on Indian educational history and philosophy
- Policy documents on national and global education reforms
- Research literature on digital pedagogy and educational technology
- Studies on inclusive and multilingual education
- Works on teacher education, leadership, and professional ethics
- Global reports on education and the future of work

These readings complement the book by offering theoretical depth, comparative insights, and applied perspectives.

5. Future Directions in Indian Education

The future of Indian education lies in **integrating tradition with innovation** . Key directions include:

- Strengthening research-oriented and innovation-driven education

- Expanding equitable digital infrastructure across regions
- Deepening teacher autonomy, leadership, and professional respect
- Embedding sustainability, ethics, and citizenship education
- Enhancing global collaboration while preserving cultural identity
- Promoting flexible, lifelong learning pathways
- Leveraging data-informed decision-making in educational governance

These directions position education as both a social equalizer and a catalyst for national development.

6. Summary of Key Points

- Indian education has evolved through ancient, medieval, colonial, and modern phases
- Traditional systems emphasized holistic and value-based learning
- Colonial education restructured institutions and priorities
- Post-independence reforms expanded access and nation-building goals
- Recent policies promote flexibility, inclusivity, and skill orientation
- Technology is reshaping pedagogy, access, and lifelong learning
- Teachers remain central to educational transformation
- Equity, multilingualism, and inclusion are critical for social justice
- The future demands a balance between Indian values and global competence

ABOUT THE AUTHOR

Dr. Shubhra Chaturvedi is a distinguished Professor of Teacher Education at J.V. Jain College, Saharanpur, with over 25 years of extensive experience in higher education, research, and academic leadership. She holds a Ph.D. from Dayalbagh Educational Institute, Agra, and is UGC-NET qualified, with postgraduate degrees in Political Science, Hindi, and Education. Her scholarly contributions include four authoritative books and more than thirty-five research papers published in reputed national and international journals. Her research interests span teacher education, inclusive and special education, mental health, educational technology, and NEP 2020. Dr. Chaturvedi has successfully supervised twelve Ph.D. scholars and guided over sixty M.Ed. dissertations. She is a frequent resource person, keynote speaker, and session chair at national and international seminars and conferences. Honoured by CCS University for her role in NEP 2020 implementation, she continues to contribute actively to academic innovation, research mentoring, and policy-oriented educational discourse.

10. E-LIBRAIRIE – France (French online bookstore)
11. Everand – India (Everand Book Distributor is based in India)
12. EXLIBRIS – Switzerland
13. Fable – United Kingdom (UK/Europe digital subscription book service)
14. Flipkart – India
15. GANDHI.com – Mexico (Librerías Gandhi)
16. Google Book – United States (Google LLC)
17. Google Audio Book – United States (Google LLC)
18. IBS.IT – Italy Wikipedia
19. Indigo – Canada
20. Kobo – Canada Wikipedia
21. Kindle – United States (Amazon product)
22. LAFELTRINELLI – Italy Wikipedia
23. Lehmanns – Germany
24. Lulu – United States
25. MORAWA – Austria
26. Rakuten Japan – Japan (Rakuten)
27. Smashwords – United States
28. Tolino / Thalia – Germany (Tolino is a German-language eBook ecosystem, Thalia DE)

29. Vivlio – France

30. Saxo – Denmark (Saxo.com)

31. YES24 – South Korea and others.

🎁 You will receive 20 physical author copies FREE to your Indian address.

☆ You can also receive 5 book reviews:

* 3 reviews by eminent university professors

* 2 reviews from your own group/colleagues/seniors/teachers

www.books.wissira.us

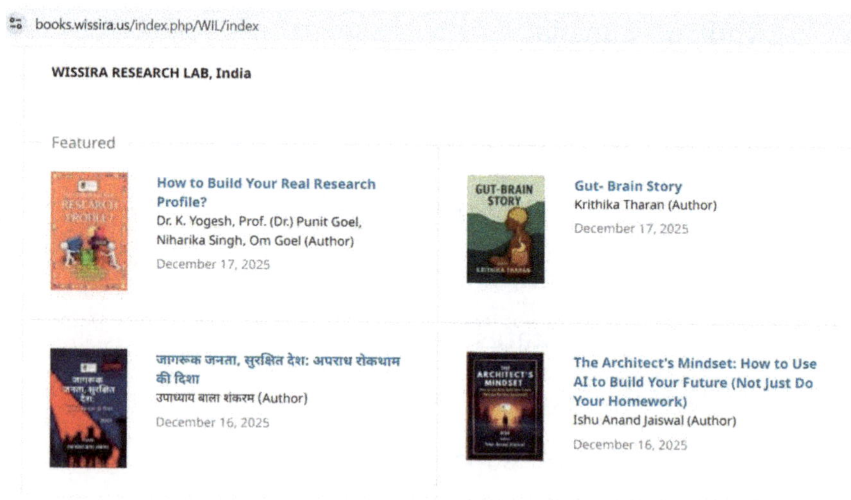

www.books.wissira.us

DOI: https://doi.org/10.63345/book.wrl.2512000324

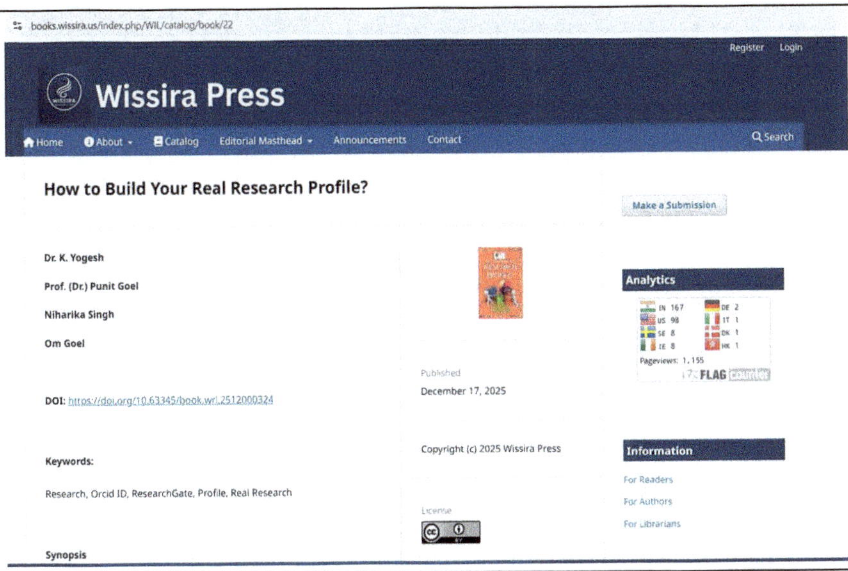

https://books.wissira.us/index.php/WIL/login

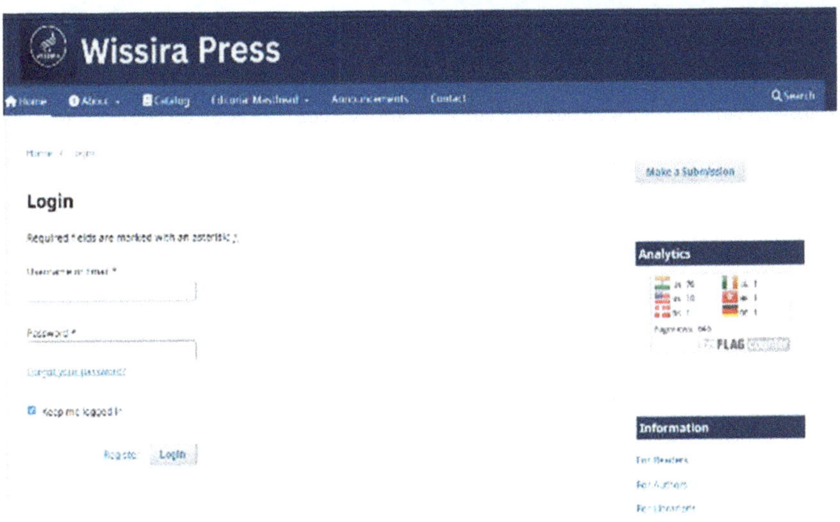

https://books.wissira.us/index.php/WIL/catalog

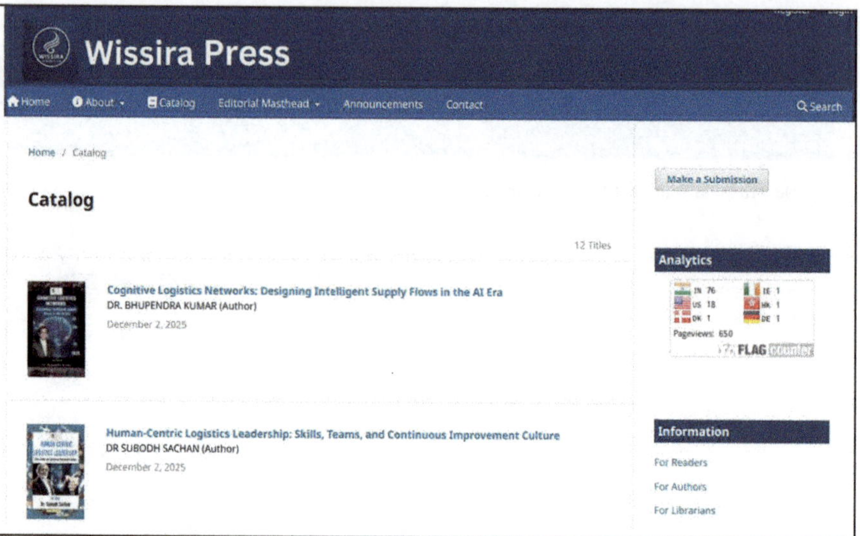

https://books.wissira.us/index.php/WIL/about/contact

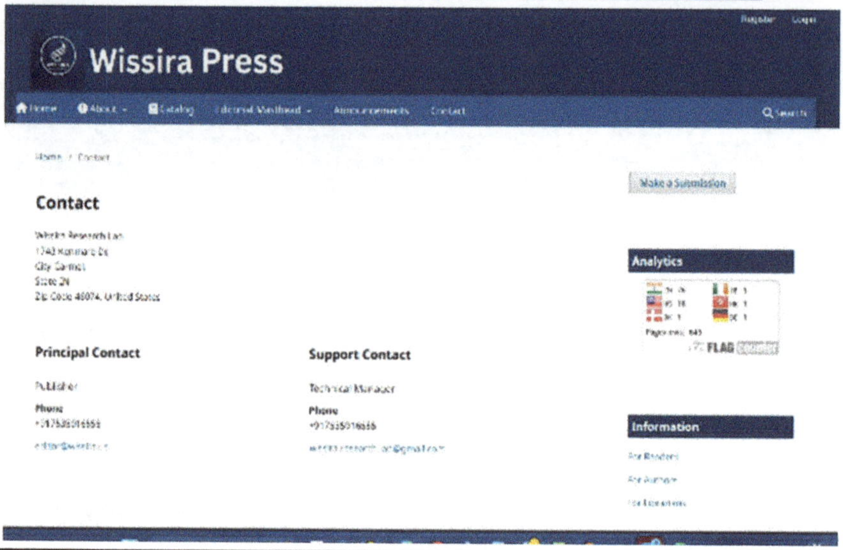

https://www.amazon.in/dp/B0G7MQFD2L

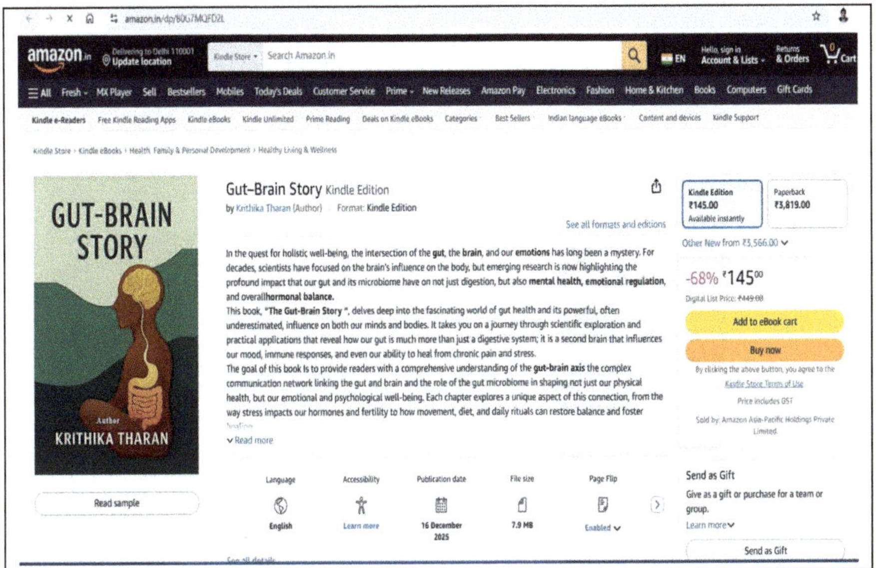

https://books.apple.com/us/book/the-architects-mindset-how-to-use-ai-to-build-your/id6756545876

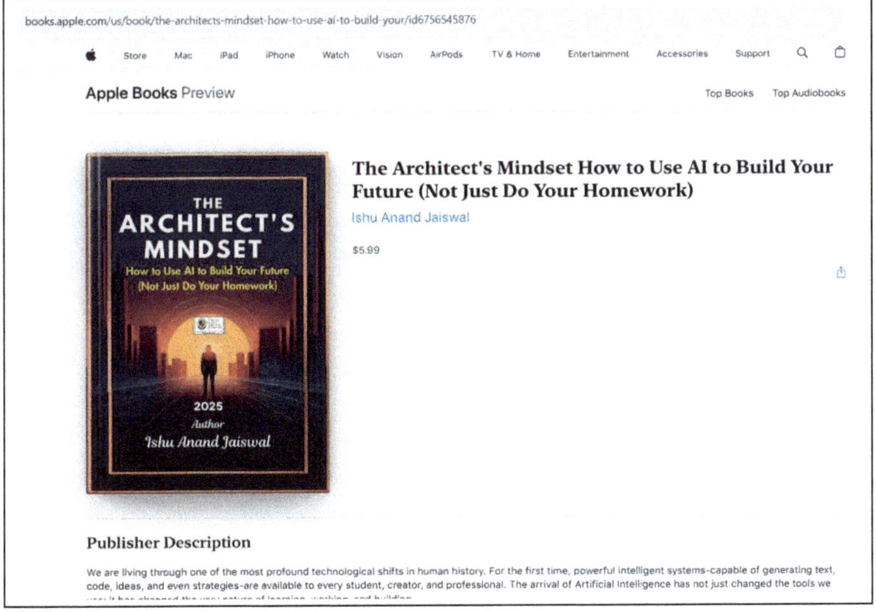

Flipkart:
https://tinyurl.com/WissieaPressBook250306Human

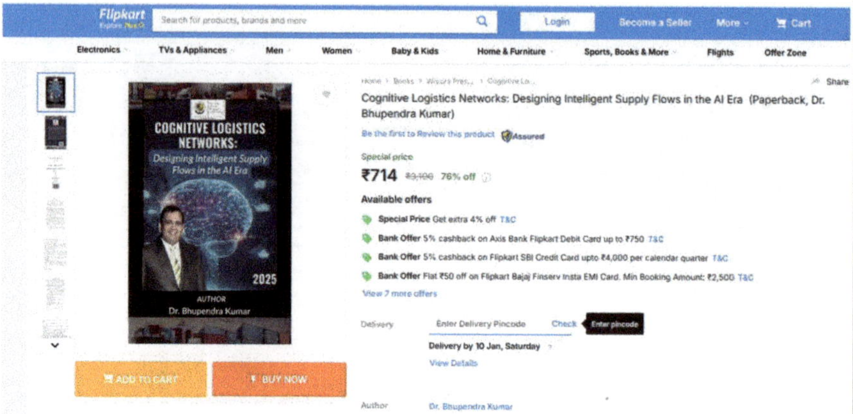

https://play.google.com/store/audiobooks/details?id=AQAAAEAa9DeoPM

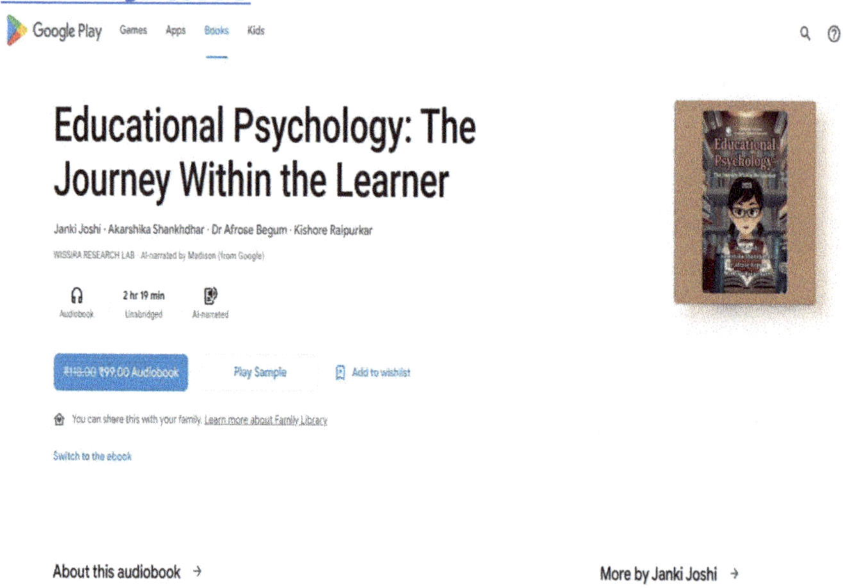

https://shop.vivlio.com/product/9798232547615_9798232547615_10020/human-centric-logistics-leadership-skills-teams-and-continuous-improvement-culture

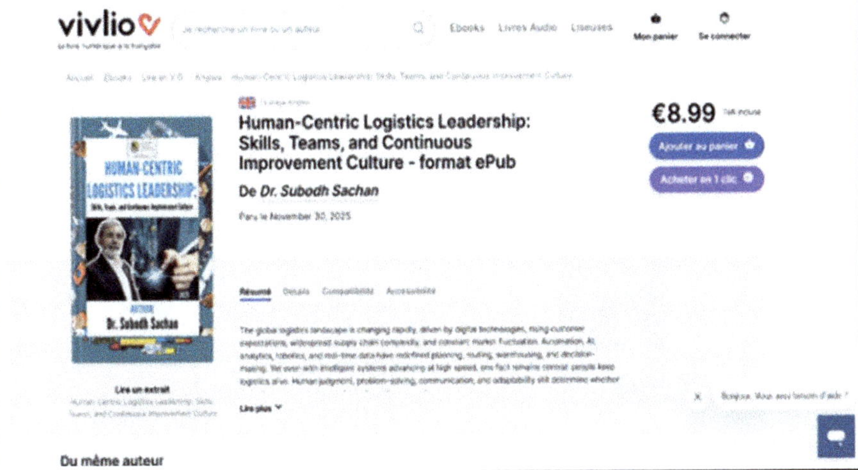

https://www.kobo.com/in/en/ebook/from-shakespeare-to-tagore-reinterpreting-english-literature-through-indian-sensibility?sId=070486d4-8aef-4220-a1d2-26bb2ba8ecb6&ssId=3FJLsnB4eTMdnS31kaTcM

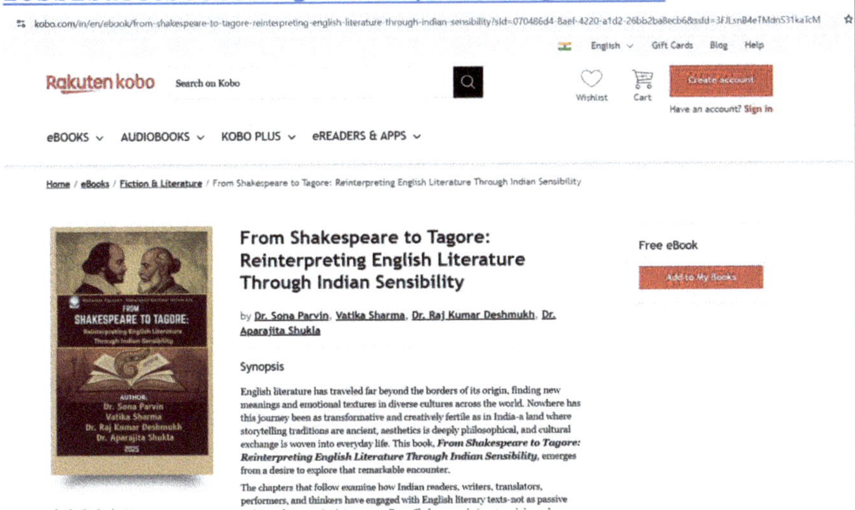

https://fable.co/book/x-9798230804772

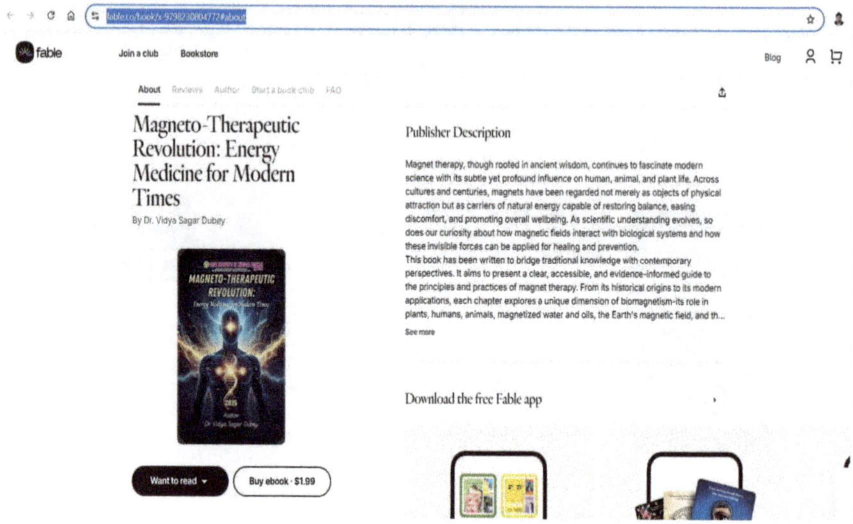

https://www.lulu.com/shop/dr-subodh-sachan/human-centric-logistics-leadership/ebook/product-rmj4erq.html?q=Human-Centric+Logistics+Leadership%3A+Skills%2C+Teams%2C+and+Continuous+Improvement+Culture&page=1&pageSize=

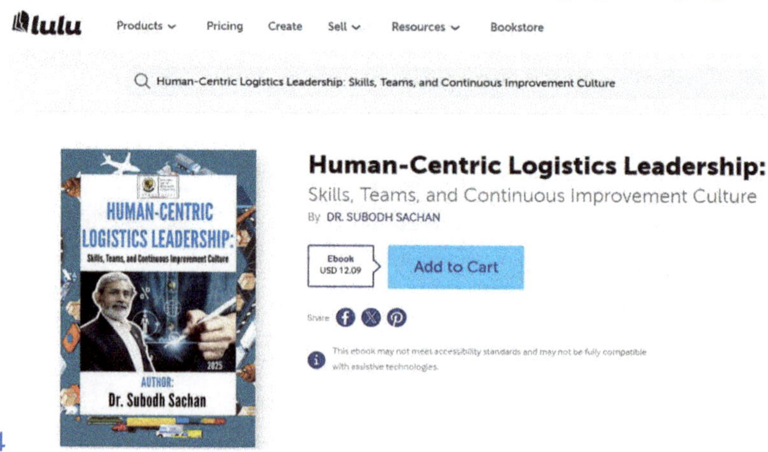

4

https://play.google.com/store/audiobooks/details?id=AQAAAEDqoRHh6M

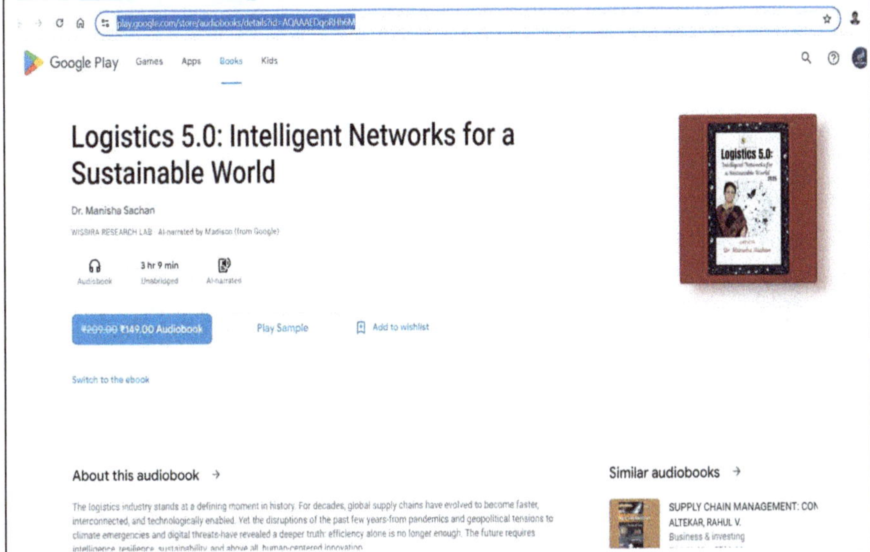

https://play.google.com/store/books/details?id=TbmfEQAAQBAJ

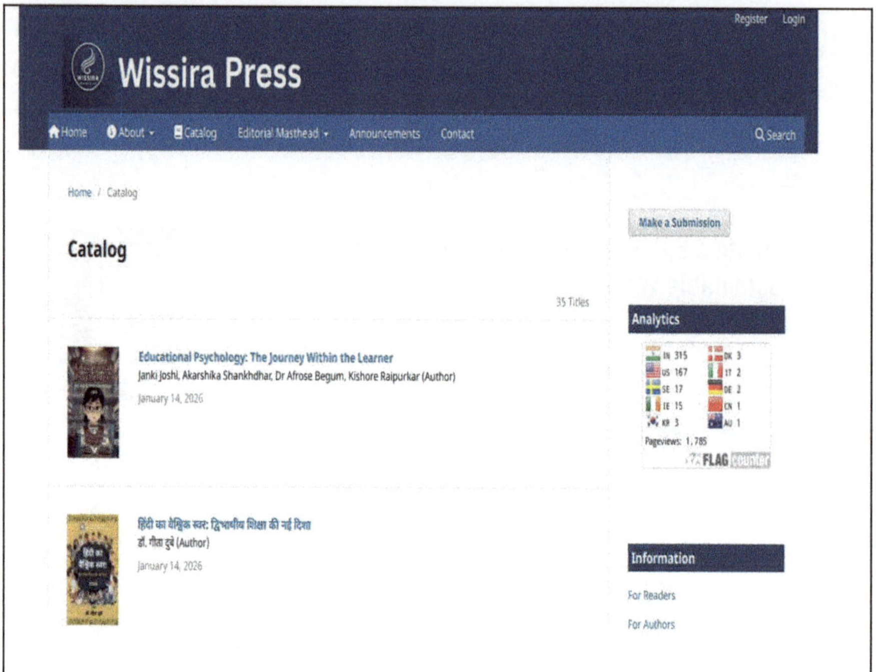

https://www.smashwords.com/books/view/1943936

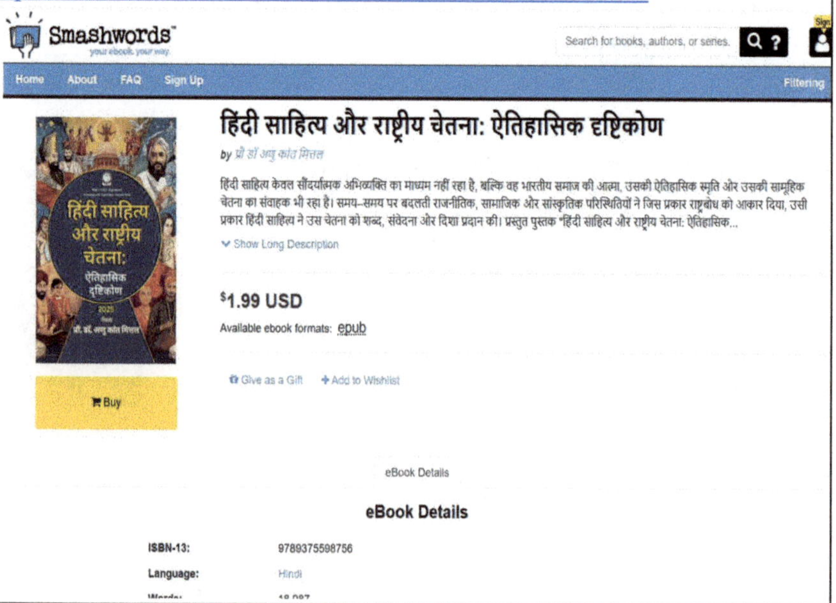

Amazon Kindle

Amazon

Flipkart

LULU

Apple Books

Barnes & Nobles

Everand

Fable

Kobo

Analytics

IN	135	IT	1
US	84	DK	1
SE	8	HK	1
IE	8	DE	1

Pageviews: 1,012

FLAG counter

Information

For Readers

For Authors

For Librarians

Keywords

sustain long-term operational excellence.

Across the nine chapters of this work, readers will find a structured and practical approach to understanding how leadership influences logistics outcomes. Beginning with the foundations of human-centric leadership, the book explores essential competencies such as communication, empathy, decision-making, and ethical responsibility-skills that enable leaders to build credibility and trust in high-pressure environments. It then moves deeper into the dynamics of teamwork, motivation, and empowerment, highlighting how resilient and collaborative teams become the backbone of

Smashwords

Tolino

Vivlio

Google Books

---

www.ingramcontent.com/pod-product-compliance
Ingram Content Group UK Ltd.
Pitfield, Milton Keynes, MK11 3LW, UK
UKHW021411190726
13845UKWH00028B/1012

9 789375 598909